"Poor Justice"

"Poor Justice"

Bob O. Parris

Writers Club Press
San Jose New York Lincoln Shanghai

"Poor Justice"

Writers Club Press
an imprint of iUniverse, Inc.

For information address:
iUniverse, Inc.
5220 S. 16th St., Suite 200
Lincoln, NE 68512
www.iuniverse.com

POOR JUSTICE is a true story. Scenes not actually witnessed by the author have been researched and represent the facts. Which is more than the jury received in this case in chief.

ISBN: 0-595-20536-4

Printed in the United States of America

Dedication

This book is dedicated to the hundreds of innocent people in the Federal Justice System.

"There is a path which no man knoweth, one which the Vulture's eye hath not seen." JOB 28.7

"FBI perjury goes on all the time. Mostly, the agent feels he has the right man, he just lacks hard evidence, so, he makes some up and we help him put the criminal away. To give everyone a fair trial would be a waste of time, energy, and money."

John Raley, former U.S. Attorney for Eastern Oklahoma

Forward

To A New Beginning of Us

In the beginning all Constitutional violations were appealable to the Supreme Court. This was changed twenty years ago. Now only one out of five thousand applications to the Supreme Court are accepted for review. The other four thousand nine hundred and ninety-nine have lost the rights guaranteed by the Constitution, and reviewed by the Supreme Court of the United States of American.

In 1973, too many criminals were going free because Law Enforcement had their hands tied in many cases, and the Court System made double certain no innocent people are found guilty of a, *jail time,* crime. More laws and additional public funds helped put two million people behind bars. With the new power and a strong desire to put every crook in prison, law enforcement begin closing loopholes and increasing their chance of gaining a conviction by enhancing the evidence with creative theories and false documentation. These activities were justified as the "Fire with Fire rational. *The criminal's are going to lie to keep their butts out of jail, so…we can do a little of that ourselves to balance things out.* As long as Law Enforcement are honest the idea of putting criminals in prison at any cost, seemed all right. What accountability exists for the dishonest Law Enforcement Officer?

The first great disappointment in my life came when those darn Russians shot down our spy plane. You remember how we all hated those rotten Communists for spying on us? To find out we were doing the same was such a horrible blow to a young kid like me. I listened to the *Lone Ranger, the Shadow, and the Green Hornet* on the Radio every week.

Justice always prevailed in the end, and those that would rob and plunder were always caught and punished. We were safe in our homes, schools, and communities. American's were the good guy's with the white hats.

We were a shinning Example of honesty and fair play to the world. Is it selected listening, or an intangible ability people have too boldly ignore facts that would impeach their opinion? Maybe we were naïve when we were Young, but what about now? Back then, I knew the County Sheriff stopped all loaded down Automobiles coming across the Arkansas border into Sequoyah County, Oklahoma.

A lot of them were straining the springs with a load of illegal whiskey. E.W. Floyd, brother of Pretty Boy Floyd, was our sheriff. He would arrest the rumrunners and impound their whiskey. The Justice of the Peace set a cash bond and the guy drove off into the sunset, without his booze. Sheriff Floyd would take the illegal whiskey over to his brother-in-law, Mike Carlton.

Mike was on a corner lot in Sallisaw. You could yell your order to Mike at the front door, drive around back, and his wife, Mary, would have your order ready when you got to the back door. Pretty Boy Floyd was a bad guy.

His body is buried about five miles down the road from where I was born. His Brother, the Sheriff, is the good guy with the white hat, right?

The Mexicans, Blacks, Indians, Irish, Italians, Jews, and Chinese, have all taken turns in the barrel. During the last one hundred years, they have all bullied each other. Today, the *Poor* continue to be abused. Why is it, in our society, part of bettering ourselves depends on how much farther down we can beat those beneath us?

With the help of my family and a lot of nice folks in Sequoyah and Adair Counties, I made it up to near the top of the political ladder. The view from that point made me want to repeal some laws making everything we do a crime and allowing Law Enforcement Employees discretion as to which laws they would enforce. Safety belts save lives, but to penalize someone stupid enough not to hook them up is against my creed. Smoke detectors also save lives, but do you want people coming into your home making sure you are saving your life? And, make you pay a fine if you are caught not saving your life?

How about breaking your door down at two o'clock in the morning to serve a summons? It has always been my opinion; people go in and out of their homes on a regular basis. Why not wait until they are going to the store or church, then get em? What could they be doing in their homes that would be so urgent that it had to be in the public's interest to stop it before dawn? It would be great if everyone took the moral high ground, like me? We could quit wasting time writing moral laws and filling up the prisons.

Rep. Cleta Dethridge is now married to Dale Mitchell and a Newly made Republican. In 1975, Democrat Representative Cleta Dethridge (from Norman, Oklahoma) wanted to pass a law requiring all sex between people not married to each other have a written agreement for such activity. That way if a boy did it to a girl without her written permission, the boy could be charged with rape. Of course, if she signed the contract, the girl would have no recourse, should she get mad at him later.

The debate centered on whether or not the boy or the girl should carry the sex contract agreement, and when the appropriate time would be for the pin and paper to enter into the discussion. It was a fun time to be alive.

Nine or ten Democrat's were so conservative that Speaker, Bill Willis, had to worry they would all change parties and give the Republicans a majority of members in the House of Representatives.

In the 1960's too few criminals were going to jail. In 1970 the turning point begin and by 1980 there was a fairly good balance between making sure people received a fair trial and getting the criminal's off the street. In 1990 Law Enforcement gained too much of an upper hand, and thousands of poor innocent people begin being convicted. The guilty rich are still getting off; if convicted they get a honey of a sentence.

In 1970, The Court appointed the poor people a lawyer from those in regular practice. It was kind of like the luck of the draw. A defendant might get the best lawyer available in the area or someone people with money would never hire in a million years. In 1980, the "Public Defender Systems" was enacted and changed all that. Now every time a poor person gets a lawyer no person with money would hire. The Court System is backed up with inmates filing collateral attacks on their convictions, claiming incompetent assistance of counsel. Competent legal assistance is guaranteed by the Constitution of the United States of America. The Public Defender system guaranteed 98% of those charged with a crime will go to jail, *Guilty or Not*. The Public Defender is usually incompetent. In some cases the lack of funds to match the Federal Prosecutor *helps to make* him appear that way.

To be fair we should set a fee for legal services and the Court's pick the Public Defender in all criminal cases. Lawyers coming out of College could go to the Prosecutors office, the Public Defenders office, or, on their own in Civil Court practice, Family practice, or Business Law. If the Defendant has money he pays the legal fee. If he has no money, the Government pays the fee. That way everyone would have an equal opportunity under the law. And, the conviction rate would go from 98% to 100%. Even the Rich would get equal justice under the law. I would be willing to wager the rich people in our society would get more money appropriated for the public defender's office, and less for the Prosecutor's Office. Where would O.J. be today if the Judge had appointed him a public defender? The Cost to convict a poor citizen of the U.S. has gone from $19,000 in 1970 to less than $12,500 in 2000. (This rate is determined without using high profile cases where real lawyers make millions—such as the Oklahoma City Bomber and his buddy. They never got a public defender.) Defending poor people's freedom is the only thing that has gone down in the last thirty years?

"What's up with that?"

If you don't agree with this solution to the Problem, how about letting the Special Agent's take the person they feel broke the law out to the Prison and check him/her in? The Warden could look up the amount of time to serve, from the guidelines, and hold him for that long. Sound silly? Try what we have now. By eliminating the expense of an unfair trial we could save big bucks. Seventy-three percent of potential jurors say - "they wouldn't have brought him into Court if he wasn't guilty." If the FBI claims you are guilty, you might as well pack your bags. $50,000 for a real lawyer will improve your chances.

Without having to worry about the Supreme Court becoming involved, prosecutors are in a position to use illegal means to gain a conviction. It appears to me, from looking at thousands of cases, only 15% of public defender (poor) cases are published. Those cases not being published cannot be used as "Dictum, or for supersedeas relief motions." Non-Published case's conflict with settled law and there are no standards even among those cases. The usual conflict is within the discretion of each Judge. Length of sentence and discovery issues are second and third in the number of times they are abused.

In 1978, there were enough laws on the books to put ever man, woman, and child, in America behind bars, at least, once. So, why clutter up the books with anymore? I say let's start a new version of this great Country. Where we make every possible effort to keep innocent people out of prison? We should repeal a few of the freedom sucking moral laws written after 1980.

Let's Face the fact that people are weak and sinful, and keep our Government from making it against the law. We are putting twelve out of every Hundred poor American's behind bars, for non-violent crimes. It's costing us billions of dollars a year. Over a thousand American's and around three hundred Mexican citizens are in a Federal Prison, and they can prove they are innocent (i.e. if they had the chance of presenting their case to a human being.) That's a disaster and a shame that will come back to haunt us some day.

Let's return to those days of our founding mother and father's. Let's leave as much freedom with the village we live in, the families we belong too, and the states we are united with.

Ever wonder how many people we would have to let out of jail to become the second nation with the most people in prison?

I don't think we should be proud of the fact that it's costing ten billion dollars a year to keep drug users and non-violent people in prison.

Get involved, do something. Send a message to our Children that life *is more special than anything else is*. Killing someone is no way to settle a disagreement. Death is not a punishment it is taking something that God gave. Make a pledge to become a difference maker in your community. Let your creed and not your greed become your need.

I voted for the death penalty in Oklahoma in 1976, and I want to take that vote back.

Oklahoma Headlines

Final Edition   Oklahoma City, Oklahoma   April 29, 1978

CLOCK UNCOVERED KILLING WATER BILL

Oklahoma City (UPI) -

Shortly after 5 p.m. Friday Rep. Bob Parris, D-Sallisaw, pulled the flag that was covering the clock, ending the 1978 Legislative session, and any chances of passing a water transfer bill this year.

Legislators were surprised when the debate on Gov. David L. Boren's water bill was interrupted with a point of order call.

A sine die adjournment resolution had been passed Thursday, setting the adjournment at 5 p.m. Friday.

Parris said the time to end the Governor's arm twisting had arrived.

"We've been trying to get water to homes in my district for twenty years. The Governor wants to ship it 300 miles across the state. I am in favor of water development, so long as we begin in where the water is and work our way out to where its not."

The House had voted down the water bill on Thursday, but it was kept alive for further consideration by the joint conference committee.

Friday it passed the senate and at 4:20 p.m., and was back in the House on final passage.

BOREN HAD concentrated his efforts the last few days of the session on the water transfer plan, which was the center of a scanty legislative program.

Rep. Draper, who was presiding at the time, noticed the point of order was well taken and ruled "it is indeed 5:00 p.m., and this session of the Legislature is adjourned sine die."

Gov. Boren and Rep. Bob O. Parris

Rep. Parris said he had to stop the session before they could vote because "the Governor has promised roads, bridges, jobs, and anything that's not nailed down to get votes."

At first, Gov. Boren ordered the Oklahoma Highway patrol to bring the House Members back, then gave up.

1

Charging for a thing you do is always a good idea. Failing to do so undermines the value of your service. When you send a bill you are saying I am worth this much for the work I have done. When you are paid, everyone is clear and up to date.

For the tenth time in the last fifty-five minutes, I am on the phone calling my stockbroker, Elton Rambin, at A.G. Edwards & Sons in Fort Smith, Arkansas. It is ten in the morning and I am very nervous. Financially, for my friends and I, this will forever be equal to the stock market crash of 1929.

"Any word?" I asked

"No, still not opened. The board says news pending. If it's good news you people could double your money." He said.

"Yes, but if it's bad, I die. Tell you what, there is no way the Investment Company should be in a stock this volatile, in the first place, so, sell it on the open."

"You can get hurt entering a market order." He said.

"Sell all 5,000 shares on the open." I said.

A bad feeling, about this stock, begin making me crazy yesterday afternoon and this morning I woke up feeling the pressure even more. The urgency to sell was chewing my insides up.

"I Just want to be rid of it." I added.

Yesterday the stock had been as high as $37.50. I placed an order to sell at $38.00. It never got that high, before going back down to $35.00 at the close. The Investment Company would make a profit of $20,000, if the stocks were sold at $35.00. The Company would only be down $10,000 for the three year's I have been portfolio manager. If I could just get this Company even I am getting away from it. Only loan money or give investment advice to personal friends if you are ready to lose them.

"You need to keep your shirt on and let this stock grow a little. Give it some time." Eldon said.

"I'm going to the office. Sell the stock, if it opens for trading. Call me right away, if there is any news at all."

Three years of being in quick sand because of this Investment Company has been more than a pain in the butt. The original deal was easy: I contracted to invest in preferred stock in 1980 and sell it in 2005. The stock I purchased was to pay 12% during this period. How much work would that have been? Buy it-put it in the lock box for twenty-five years—pull it out and sell it.

For three years I have spent more time worrying about this investment company than anything else, and I am not charging anything for it. Lawyers call what I am doing for the eleven owners of the Investment Company, *pro bono* (working for free). To me, it has meant I was a *bonehead* for making such a deal.

Until five years ago, I could do no wrong. Every trade in the stock market made money. Buildings, land, options, everything I purchased was profitable. I ran for election nine times and won eight. The idea someone up there was helping gave me a wonderful feeling in my bones.

Eleven of my Accounting customers were doing so well financially, from taking my advice; they were in a high tax bracket. Forming a trust taxed as a Corporation appeared to be the best way to shelter some of their higher income and lower the tax bite. The Corporation (trust) could operate without adding to the Individual's Taxes. When everyone was slowing down in twenty-five years or so, the money could be removed and the profit would be Fifty- Percent tax-free. During the twenty-five years the Corporation would be receiving dividends from another Corporation Eight-five percent tax-free. Best of all, the prime rate in 1980 was 12%. The Company would be able to lock-in this high interest rate for the next twenty-five years. It was a good idea and if the owners of the Company would have stayed with the objectives, things would have turned out great, and I would be a hero instead of feeling such pain.

Yes, *Locking in* the high interest rate and postponing taxes for the next twenty-five years were the goals. I invested $38.00 per share in OG&E Pf. 5.00, Georgia Power cost $36.50, also pays $5.00. And, Humana Pf 2.50 cost $18.00 per share and, of course, they paid $2.50 every year. These companies were selling a twenty-five year note and calling it "preferred stock." In the year 2005, OG&E and Georgia Power will buy back their stock at $50.00. In 2005, Humana will pay $25.00. Between 1980 and 2005, these companies will pay the dividend. None of this is subject to change as is common stock on the stock market. The owners invested $450,000 in their Investment Company. I invested the money for them and put the stock certificates in a lock box. A person wouldn't charge much for an easy deal like this. Then it started. Mrs. Milligan wanted $80,000 of her money back after only six months. She removed another $40,000 of her long-term investment three months later.

Of course, I had to sell some of the stock at a loss to return her money. When interest rates go up the price of preferred stock goes down. This is why you never buy them on a short-term basis. When Mr. Jackson removed $52,500 to purchase a house, I was forced to sell even more stock at a time when the prime rate was 18%. Later, Mrs. Milligan brought the money back she had removed plus the profit she had made on it. I had to find other kinds of stock to buy, because the interest rates were coming back down, just as we all knew they would, eventually.

Had there been a freeze on the account for the first two years. Or, if the owners had been required to pay a penalty for early withdrawal, the Company would be worth $560,000 in 1982, and $627,200 in 1983. Instead, I have all this extra aggravation, and the Company being down $30,000. And, I'm on the phone screaming at Eldon Rambin.

In 2001, the Investment Company would have been worth 3.4 Million dollar's. The gain would have been 85% tax free to the Company over the twenty-year period, and a 50% tax-free capital gain to the owner/investors. The only risk was Georgia Power, Humana, or OG&E, might fail. In which case the preferred stock would be paid off ahead of the common stock.

"Eldon, what's happening? Is the stock still on hold, sold, being sold, or what?"

Well, the stock opened down five buck about fifteen minutes ago. I'm just waiting for it to take a little bounce before I put the order in." Eldon said.

"Are you kidding me? What's wrong with you? Don't screw around with me, Eldon, I already told you to sell the damn shit. I know you know how to do it. Please, just sell it, Okay?" Please.

"It's off another buck, I would recommend we hold a little longer. It's gonna go back up." he said.

"Are you hard hearing or something? Forget about the advice! You got me in this stupid stock and I already told you to sell it, now do it. Sell it, or, I am driving to Ft. Smith and make your lip as fat as your sorry fat ass. You understand that?"

I slammed the phone down and begin stomping around the office muttering to myself and calling Eldon every bad name I could think of. How could I have let this happen? I'm able to see what I should have done. The problem is what should I do now? My God this is a nightmare.

In 1980, the present day mutual fund business was just beginning. The Tax Code had to be changed because Public Accountants were discovering loopholes in Public trust laws allowing large sums of money to grow tax-free. How could such a good idea turn out to be so wrong?

I am the first to blame, it was my idea, but three of the other owners are a factor in the loss. They (or I) should never have allowed early withdrawals without a penalty. Not having an Annual Audit was Bill Ford's fault and he is the only one to blame for that error. The owners should have insisted on Bill Ford hiring a public accountant to perform the annual audit, as required by Oklahoma's public trust laws. Not doing it allowed for us all to continue dreaming and hoping for better times just around the corner. The next trade would be the big one.

2

The 12% interest rate the owners were so excited about in 1980 became very unattractive when the prime rate went to 18% in 1981, and set a record high of 21.5% in 1982. Looking at it today, how many people would like to be getting that kind of interest on their money? Looking at it back then, people worried how much higher it would go.

In early 1983, interest rates of 12% were back to being a fairly good rate again. The Investment Company had been forced to sell some stock at a loss and now it would cost more than before to purchase it back. Which proves had we kept the original goal of twenty-five years, not only would we have not lost $30,000, we would be ahead of the 12% income by around $19,000.

What do you think I should we do? I asked one of the owners almost weekly. We know OG&E, Humana, and Georgia

Power stock are going back up when the interest rates turn around, right? (I am looking for guidance from the owner's). What do you think? Should we take our loss and get out? As the owners of the Investment Company came by my Office, we discussed these future investments. They knew how many shares of stock the company has, and the price they paid. They know today's price as well as yesterdays. They know the phone number of Eldon Rambin at A.G. Edwards & Sons. My only responsibility is to accept, invest, and return the money. That's it. All this helps very little, as I think about the growing loss we are suffering.

"The Interest Rates can't go any higher." Eldon would say. "You guy's are in this for the long haul." would be another reply. "Only a couple of dollars has been lost on each stock, things will turn around," was the answer the Stock Broker gave me most of the time.

In October of '83, the prime rate came back down to 12% and was going lower. Mrs. Milligan reinvested the $120,000 she had removed, plus the $43,000 profit she made on the money. I invested the new money in Oil Stocks paying a good dividend and selling options in order to make the 12%.

I believed oil stock was going to go up over the long term. For the next four years I was wrong. The following fourteen years (1987 to 2001), I was correct. One of the oil stocks I purchased was Mobil Oil Company at $40.00 per share. The annual dividends were $5.00 and I sold $45.00 options for a $1.00 per share. The six dollars per year on an investment of $40 made the guarantee of twelve percent. Record Interest Rates killed us in '80, '81, and '82. Now, Record Low Oil prices are going to take us further down. The price of oil dropped from $48.00 dollars a barrel to $10.00. And, *"under the circumstance"* Mobil Oil Company holding at $30.00 is *"fine."* I ask Bill Ford… "What should we do? Mobil Oil is down ten dollars, do you think it will go up or down from here?"

"I don't know! Do what you think best." Bill said.

The Stock goes back up to $33.00 and I am happy. Then, It goes back down to $29.00 and I am sad. Up and Down, that is what the Stock Market does.

I don't think everything should be blamed on me. Maybe a $30,000 loss isn't to bad considering the circumstance of long-term investments, and short-term selling. I made no contract to find investments making 12% after 1984 because none could be found.

Eldon Rambin told me this Oil Company was about to complete a huge new discovery in the Anadarko basin. He said they own mineral rights to over 255,000 acres in the area.

"It's gonna be big." Yesterday he looked good, but not today.

Thirty Thousand dollars down and the desire to get back even helped me decide to take a chance. Do something big and catch up. A break is definitely due. I can't get anything else done for worrying about this Company I have helped get my friends involved in. Yesterday, the future looked bright. Twenty Thousand of the Thirty had been made back, with only Ten to go. Now, I am facing an additional loss. Why didn't I take yesterdays profit and be happy? I asked myself as I picked up the phone and called A.G. Edwards & Sons in Fort Smith, Arkansas.

"All right Eldon what did we get for the damn stock?"

"Bob, you are just not going to believe this. The stock has dropped another few dollars. The bid is only $25.00 a share." Eldon said.

All the air went out of me. Had I not been setting down, I would have fell to the floor. "It is unimportant to me how much the stock is now, what I what to know is how much it was sold for?"

"I put the order in at $30.00 and it didn't get there... yet."
Eldon said. (This is all happening before Computers allowed
us to keep track of our stock on an almost instant basis. Today,
I could enter a trade and know the results within minutes). It
really was a good thing Eldon Rambin was in Ft. Smith, and I
was in Sallisaw. Otherwise I would have seriously maimed the
son-of-a-bitch.

"Eldon hear me good. Sell the stock. Sell the stock,
please...just do it now. Sell the stock. Do you hear me?"
"Please sell the stock immediately and any price you can get."

"Okay, I am doing it right now, hold on. I'm changing the
limit order of $30.00 to a market order. Okay, okay, there, it's
in. Give it about three minutes and it cross the ticker. The last
trade was twenty-two dollars. 5,000 shares just sold for
twenty. It's only been two minutes, but it could be us. Wait,
my God, there goes 2,000 shares at $16.00. Okay, hold on here
comes 3,000 shares at $10.00 and there is some more at nine
dollars. Stopped, trading has stopped."

The great stock recommended by Eldon Rambin cost
$155,000. Now the Investment Company sold it back for
$39,000. My mouth will not move... it is dry and locked. I
feel weak all over. After a long period of time I am finally able
to say: "I'm filing Court action against you and A.G. Edwards
tomorrow. You are a sorry bastard. You have cost us over a
hundred thousand dollars."

So much of a lost in one morning is unimaginable. The
official fills came back twenty minutes later. We sold 3,000
shares at $10.00, and 1,000 at $9.00. The remaining 1,000
shares are in my file cabinet at the writing of this book, and
they are worthless. Over and over, I ask the same question:
"What do I do *now*?"

The loss is far too great to continue. Sell everything I have and try to make up the difference, is the only answer. I can't let my friends down.

On January 1, 1984, the owners have lost $223,000 in the Investment Company. If I liquidate I can raise almost that much? If I sell my Accounting Business for $100,000.00, and get half down, sell two building worth in excess of $100,000 for $75,000, and sell a piece of land south of Sallisaw for $35,000. I could return enough to close out this unbelievable affair and hopefully feel better about my part in it.

3

It seemed strange the day Bill Ford came by my office. I had just finished calculating each persons loss and was in the process of typing up a detailed accounting for them to look at, when Mr. Ford said James Trudeau (Mrs. Milligan's son-in-law) was going to purchase his auto parts store for $400,000. He wanted to know how much tax he would have to pay. "You could figure about 50% because you don't have much cost in the business and your wife's salary takes up all your deductions, and puts anything you make in a higher tax bracket."

"Oh shit, Bill said, anyway I can get out of that?"

We had a long discussion about getting paid in installments instead of a lump sum and stuff like that. Then I told him: If he traded his business for stock in his Investment Company, instead of selling it for cash, he could save half of the sale price on his tax return until he sold the stock.

When James Trudeau came around and asked me if I thought Mr. Ford's parts business was worth that much? I lied to him because I felt the way it happened it was money that could help Mrs. Milligan, and Bill Ford's, company gain enough money to make up the loss. Mrs. Milligan's $500,000 gift to her daughter, Mary Jo Milligan Trudeau, would assist in rebuilding Mrs. Milligan's Company. Bill Ford could think he got $400,000 for a business worth $100,000. Bill took out $90,000 and reported that amount on his 1984 tax return. Everything Mr. Ford had in his auto parts business had been fully depreciated. The building belonged to J.C. Shockey. His only asset was the business name, some shelving, and inventory valued at $35,000 (cost). I would say Mr. Ford's business was worth little more than the $90,000. Mr. Ford took $90,000 in cash and 310 shares of beneficial interest in the Investment Company.

Mr. Ford made a "home run," as they say in the car business, when you get your price for the Car you sold and have the trade-in free and clear. Or, as my daddy would say, Bill Ford got a "free roll." I think its safe to say he got the best of the deal. With Wal-Mart moving into town, just down the street, Mr. Ford's business was only going to be worth less and less as time passed. James used the money Mrs. Milligan gave to Mary Jo for the purchase and the stock Mrs. Milligan had in the Investment Company was to go the Mary JO's children upon Mrs. Milligan reaching the age of 75.

In a short span of time Mr. Trudeau changed the name from Bill's Auto Supply to Doc's Auto Supply. A little later he gave half the Store back to Mr. Ford just to get him to come in and work part time to help get the business back from Wal-Mart.

Mrs. Milligan also gave her son, Billy Trudeau, land in Mississippi valued at more than $500,000. Before giving all this away, Mrs. Milligan was a millionaire. When she first came to Sallisaw, she was getting Social Security and $90.00 a month from stocks her husband had purchased. She had 30-year bonds that brought in nothing for the next twenty years. The stocks and bonds were traded for current income investments producing $1,323 per month in 1978. In 1980 Mrs. Milligan was paying $500 per month to her church. The most she ever had in her investment company at any time was $292,000.

In late 1983, I told Mrs. Milligan she should divest herself of some of her money or the Government would get it when she went to the nursing home. A person having $2,000 or less gets the nursing home paid by Medicare; otherwise, it would cost her $2,125 per month. I don't know what the illness was, but all her sister's had come down with it and spent a lot of time in the nursing home before they died. I think she believed she was going to get it at around seventy-five. Otherwise why would a seventy-year-old person want a long-term investment?

Just as record high interest rates cost the Company in '82 and '83, so did the price of oil ruin the Company in 1984-86. The Company was lucky to have $331,000 left in the account, when I left on May 16, 1986. The price of oil went from a high of $48.00 dollars a barrel in 1984, to a record low of $10.00 in 1986. The Company should have lost 75% of its value.

With two record breaking events working against the Company, I had no chance. Later, Special Agent Tom Vest was unable to understand where the $26.00 dollars went.

He said, "Where is the $26.00?"

"What $26.00 are you talking about?"

"You bought Mobil Oil stock for $40.00 a share and sold it for $24.00. Where is the $26.00?" Vest wanted to know. I made several different kinds of attempts to tell him how it was in the Stock Market somewhere, but he never understood.

After I sold my Accounting Business in August of '84, I built a car dealership. The first half of 1985 the car business made good money. Profits went flat during the last half of 1985, and were doing poorly the first four months of 1986. On May 10, 1986, GMAC brought Sixteen repossessed cars onto my Car Lot. The value dropped from our sales price of $255,000 to a new floor plan value of $102,000. On the morning of May 16, 1986, Nineteen more repossessed cars and trucks were brought in, and a fat old gal from GMAC came into my office and demanded a check for $278,000 dollars. I advised her the sale of cars and trucks were "approved by GMAC," on a "No Recourse" basis. My contract with GMAC says these cars could be on my lot, I will attempt to sell them, but they belonged to GMAC.

"When GMAC accepts the customer's purchase, I'm done with it." I said.

"You don't pay the money and I haul every car off your lot, simple as that." the fat gal said.

GMAC picked up all my new and used vehicles and hauled them off. I locked up the building and front gate and went home.

The suppliers and employees were paid (everyone except GMAC). It is May 16, 1986, and I now have lost everything I have.

I call the chairman of the Investment Company, Bill Ford, and tell him I would no longer be able to manage the Company's portfolio. The next day, GMAC went to the Courthouse and filed a civil suit asking for payment of all the new cars they had hauled off, plus they wanted payment for the repossessions. While I was out of the State, GMAC obtained default judgment in the amount of 2.7 million dollars. This was later set aside and eventually GMAC paid me $40,000 of the more than $350,000 loss they caused me.

On May 16, 1986, at 4:28 p.m., the Investment Company's $331,000 was turned over the Mr. Ford to continue managing or divide amount with the other owners.

"Use this to take care of Milligan, Jackson, Farmer, Ware, Settle, Lee, and Brooks. I will take care of Carol, Mother, and Melba. I said.

Bill Ford put all the money in his pocket and got the other owners to help him pay Attorney, Jim Jones, to sue me for the $300,000 they alleged I diverted to my personal use.

My mother lost $50,000 in this Company. My Wife, Carol, lost $30,000 and my grandmother put $25,000 in the Investment Company for me, as my part of my inheritance. I lost that and around $32,000 more. Looking back I see the *Things I should have done*: (a) I should have stopped trying back in 1982. (b) I should have used my assets to make up the Company's loss and stopped in 1983. (c) I should have told Trudeau he could purchase the Auto Parts business from Bill Ford for $90,000, why pay more? (d) I should have made A.G. Edwards & Sons pay for Eldon Rambin's failure to sell the stock, as I ordered. (e) On May 16, 1986, I should have been man enough to face my former friends and hand each one of them 50% of there money back. (f) Bill Ford removed $90,000 from the Company in 1984, and only had $85,000 remaining (on a cash basis), when he took the entire amount of $331,000. (g) This amount included the $32,000 Mrs. Milligan deposited on April 29, 1986. Bill Ford should never have received more than he invested in the Company. I have a one million-dollar fidelity insurance policy covering "Accounting Liability and Investment Advisor." Maybe everyone can get the money back that way. Another $331,000 would get everyone his or her original investment back and I would get the $25,000 my grandmother left for me.

As part of the policy, I am unable to help the owner's collect the money. And, while nothing has been illegal with the investments, and I lost money along with the others, I am the person most responsible for the loss.

My Lawyer, Harry Scoufos, believes they might collect from the Insurance Company, and I am hoping they can, even if it makes me look guilty of a criminal offense.

For some reason, Attorney Jim Jones never included the Insurance Company in the Court Action he filed on June 3, 1986.

Mr. Scoufos sent Jim Jones a copy of a letter he wrote to my Insurance Company advising them of the lawsuit and that they may have to enter the case. The Insurance Company wrote back and said they would only become part of the case, if they were included as a codefendant. "It is a *claims made policy*," their person said, "we only consider paying people when a claim is made." Jones never filed a claim against them.

I think he knew I never intentionally lost my money and that of my friends in the stock market. So, he must have been afraid Bill Ford, would have to give up part of the $331,000. Of course, the court action ended in failure because no money was diverted to me. It was lost in the stock market and there is no insurance made that will insure the Stock Market. You can *hedge, rollover, and cover*, too help reduce the risk of stock going down in value, but that's all. Fidelity Insurance, FDIC, SIPC, Life, Accident, and Health, are examples of Insurance you can purchase. Live Births, living to a ripe old age, and loss of funds in the Stock Market, are examples of Insurance you cannot buy. What if someone told you, for $500 they could guarantee your next baby would be born alive? Or, for $2,000 they would guarantee you would live to be 134 years old? Or, how about, give me $5,000 and I will guarantee you I will double it in the stock market for you in ten days? That's crazy, right?

4

My wife, Carol, raised, bred, and raced Greyhounds. From May 1986 through April 1991, I looked for a job, helped her, and managed to send my mother $500 a month. Had I been able to find work, I was going to send my Aunt Melba her $1,384.21. In addition, I would have sent my cousin, Bill Ed, as much extra money as I was able to earn. In my mind, morally I owed them and if I ever get the chance I would pay.

Until April 1991, I would have handed the other owners of the company as much extra money as I might be able to make. The Civil Court Action in June of '86, was fine. James Trudeau lost the $400,000 Mrs. Milligan gave his wife in less than a year. He may feel he owes Mary Jo part of that money, if he ever makes any extra.

The Investment Company lost $600,000 in the Stock Market, and the additional $331,000 when Bill Ford kept the account balance on May 16, 1986. I could never find full time employment during this period of time, thanks to the FBI following me around. The FBI dropped by the places I interviewed for employment and tell the Manager,

"Parris beat two old ladies out of two million dollars, do you want to hire a guy like that?"

Helping Carol didn't pay much more than room and board. Sending my mother money lowered my saving account a little each month.

April 17, 1991, was a bright spring morning. I had suffered for five years and was beginning to feel better about myself, when the assistant U.S. Attorney and Special Agent, Tom Vest, knocked on the door at my home in Sallisaw, Oklahoma.

"Your case will be taken to the grand jury Monday." Tom Vest said.

I said, "I told you I never mailed that credit application for the Airplane."

"This is more serious than that, you may appear and testify or you don't have too, it's up to you." Vest said.

I looked at the indictment, "what the hell is this, I was cleared of the investment thing by U.S. Attorney, Roger Hilfinger, two years ago." I said.

In 1988, Mr. Hilfinger told me the investigation was over and he was not going to ask for an indictment.

"We got a new U.S. Attorney and you are back in the hot seat." Vest replied.

I read the five-page indictment while they stood watching. "You got the wrong bank account. In 1980, a guarantee of 12% was really a low rate of interest. Prime Rate was over 18%. The false pretense you have on here is what the IRS Code is, and not false. Do you have a law against true pretense?"

"Save it for the grand jury." Vest said.

I said. "Mr. Assistant U.S. Attorney, what have you got to say about this crap?"

"You are pretty arrogant for a guy who beat two old ladies out of their life savings,"

I said, "You been listening to FBI Lies. That claim was made in civil court five years ago, and they found out different. Everyone knows the money was lost in the stock market. You guys are just a few years behind the times."

"You deliberately invested in stocks you knew were going down." Vest said.

I said. "You know how stupid that sounds? It's as hard to know which stocks will go down as those that will go up."

"Tell it to the grand jury," the Assistant U.S. Attorney said.

I said, "I will, thanks for your permission. Anyone old enough to drive to the courthouse will already know how stupid that sounds."

I was about to find out more than I ever wanted to know about our Federal Justice System.

Bill Ford went all over Sallisaw, telling people he called U.S. Senator David L. Boren in Washington and told him he had only few days left to get the guy that took down the flag and ended his Water Program.

The last deposit made to the Company was a $32,000 check from Mrs. Milligan on April 29, 1986. This Deposit was part of the $331,000 in the account when I left on May 16, 1986. As part of my "scheme to Defraud" The Indictment accused me of mailing a $32,000 check on April 29,1986, of mailing a second check for $800.00 on May 20,1986, and telling one of the owners, over the phone, "I have Insurance". The five-page Indictment went on to say the Company's Checking Account was in Sallisaw, Oklahoma. I commingled investor funds and used their money for personal items, such as paying Utilities, making house payments, purchased food,

Ect. The 85% tax-free dividends between corporations were called False Pretense. The 50% tax-free capital gains are called False Pretense. The 12% interest rate is also called False Pretense. That's it, three counts of fraud, commingling, and false pretense.

The most preposterous claim made by the Government was "Mr. Parris devised a scheme to intentionally lose his money and that of his friends in the Stock Market.

Another problem with the indictment was the commingling of funds. The Government says the $32,000 deposit was mailed to the Company Checking Account in Fayetteville, Arkansas. The Government says the Company Checking Account was in Sallisaw, Oklahoma. Which is it? If I received the check in Sallisaw and deposited it in the bank in Sallisaw, there would be no mailing of the check (no Mail Fraud). If the checking account is in Fayetteville, Arkansas, then I could not commingle funds, and the personal checks out of my personal Company Account in Sallisaw would have nothing to do with the Investment Company in Fayetteville.

The Checking Account the Government used in Sallisaw is my personal business checking account and it had lots of personal and business checks. Another thing I noticed right off was how easy it was going to be for me to present a copy of the Insurance Policy. The lady called me several days after the owners filed their civil court action.

She asked me "if we win the lawsuit how will you pay? I know you lost your money too." She said

"I have fidelity insurance, you have claimed I diverted $300,000 to my personal use. If you are able to convince a jury of that the Insurance will pay you. I lost money just like you, and you know that."

There was another kind of Insurance the Owners asked me about. When the Brokerage Account was moved from A.G.

Edwards & Sons to Merrill Lynch & Co., the Checking Account was moved from First National Bank in Sallisaw to Merrill Lynch in Fayetteville. One of the Owners asked about FDIC insurance on the amount in checking. I told them that the Securities Insurance Protective Corporation (SIPC) was *as safe* as the Government (FDIC). What idiot would tell someone buying stock in the stock market was "as safe" as anything? Everyone knows how safe investing in the Stock Market is. There are no Guarantees and no Insurance to be bought against losses in the Stock Market.

I called my lawyer, Bruce Green, in Muskogee and told him about receiving the indictment. "Bring $35,000 and we will get right on it."

I said, "I only got $5,000.00."

"You know, the Fed's got a pretty good little public defender system, maybe you should try them. I will call over to the Courthouse and see how much paperwork they have and call you back."

Twenty minutes later, Mr. Green called back and advised me there was several large boxes of evidence. You might as well forget about going to the grand jury. It would only give them additional evidence to use against you. They always get indictments when they file for them. He told me to file for the Court to appoint me an Attorney, after the indictment comes down. He just couldn't take the case for less, and he had to have half the money up front.

Craig Bryant was appointed to defend me. The Government had a sure winner. Mr. Bryant had never won a case that went to trial. People who are represented by a Public Defender are found guilty a 100% of the time in the Eastern District of Oklahoma. U.S. Attorney, John Raley, had a conviction rate of 98.8%. The only time he missed was when a real lawyer represented the defendant's. Docket's are on the first Monday of each month. For me, That would be June 3, 1991.

Before the Trial, I saw Mr. Bryant three times. The first time for 25 minutes after I entered the *not guilty* plea in April. The second time we went up to the FBI Office in the Federal Courthouse and looked at seven boxes of documents. Each of boxes contained around 10,000 sheets of paper. Mr. Bryant stipulated to all 70,000 documents (mostly meaningless scraps of paper dated before 1986).

"These are past the statute of limitations, they don't mean anything, but I don't even have to answer anything about them." I said, pointing to several thousand papers from Olde and Company. No business was conducted with Olde and Company since 1983. "Five years is the time limit. I could have robbed the Queen of England in 1983, and you would be out of luck charging me in 1991.

The Government can't go on forever investigating a person. Nothing new has been found during the past four years, but here we are five years later.

"Let me tell you, this is not going to go back ten years. Look at this, a bank statement from 1978 and here is one dated July 12, 1962." I said.

"These documents can't do any harm." Bryant said

Bryant is a short, stocky, ugly, man in his late forties. His short hair and thick eyebrow's looks like he painted them with black ink. At first glance a person might take him for an intelligent, successful businessman. After a few minutes you know he was dumber than dirt.

"They will pile these papers up in the Courtroom and act like they mean something. I want them presented to the jury one at a time and the U.S. Attorney explained to me, and the jury, exactly what they mean." I replied.

As I screamed NO, NO, NO, Bryant signed the stipulation agreement for the Government. Seventy Thousand pieces of scrap paper will now look like something real important to the jury.

The third time I met with Bryant was after I filed a motion for the Court to appoint me a new Attorney. I told His Honor, Judge Frank Howell Seay, the Attorney he appointed was not looking at my box of evidence, he had not subpoenaed any of the eight witnesses I wanted called to testify in my favor, and that Mr. Bryant has stipulated to around 70,000 pieces of scrap paper.

Judge Seay denied my motion.

On June 3, 1991, at 8:04 a.m., I arrived at the Federal Courthouse in Muskogee, Oklahoma. Craig Bryant arrived about 8:55 a.m. Three men were being sentenced, as Bryant and I stepped into Judge Seay's Courtroom. They had just changed their plea too guilty.

Last week, Mr. Bryant said, "We have until the middle of the month, because there are three trials ahead of ours."

I said, "nobody ahead of us now, are they?"

"This means we go today." Bryant said.

I said, "No way, we haven't done anything to get ready, except you stipulated to their case, we have no witnesses and you only know what the Government has told you about this case. You have no idea what the eight witnesses will say and you don't know what the value of the evidence in this box is. What really happened is a mystery to you and the Government."

"These men took the plea offer, and that is what you should have done!" Mr. Bryant said

I said, "What plea offer are you talking about?"

"Plead guilty to one count and get a one year sentence, you could get as much as three years do you understand that?" Bryant said.

I said, "Nothing has ever been said about a plea offer. I never did nothing illegal, but with no money and you defending me, I'm sure taking a one-year sentence deal."

"It's too late, the deal went off last Thursday evening, you should have let me know." Bryant said.

I said, "how the hell could I let you know? I never knew there was offer."

Within an hour, a jury was picked and at 12:00 O'clock the government called its first witness.

A couple of Court Bailiff's were talking about Washington sending in one of their "Big guns" for this case.

Who in Washington would be interested in me?

5

Federal Court—Muskogee, OK—USA

The Court: I show the Government here and the defendant and his lawyer is here. Where is your other lawyer? There you are, right there. I was looking at the table for you and you're up here. Allow me. You're standing; you need something, Mr. Raley?

(The following is just as it is in the Court Record.)

Mr. Raley: Yes, Your Honor, if it please the Court. In an effort to expedite matters, we have heretofore entered into certain stipulations concerning voluminous records and exhibits with counsel. They will be referred to here during the course of the summary testimony by Agent Vest. But at this time, Your Honor, we would like to enter into a stipulation with counsel's approval.

The Court: What stipulation is that?

Mr. Raley: It's a written stipulation, Your Honor, I'll ask the—

Mr. Anderson: I have the originals and copies here, Your Honor, If I may. Government Exhibits 80 through 82.

The Court: Can you hear?

Mr. Anderson: I'm sorry, Your Honor. Eighty is a stipulation as to the authenticity of deposition transcripts, which the parties have signed.

The Court: Well, what do you want me to do? You want me to read something to the jury?

Mr. Anderson: Yes, Your Honor, I'd like to have them read to the jury. But, the one of primary importance. Your Honor, is—

The Court: You want all of them read to the jury?

Mr. Anderson: Yes, Your Honor.

The Court: Now?

Mr. Anderson: Before the presentation of the first witness, that would be preferable, Your Honor.

The Court: You don't tell—you say that the—it's stipulated to the admissibility into evidence at the trial of any and all— No. 81—of the following described banking and financial records. And then, you just—evidently it's just hundreds of documents and you don't give any numbers for them.

Mr. Anderson: Your Honor, they're marked as Group. Exhibits Nos. 1 through 11 and they're over there on the carts.

The Court: Which is which and how are they identified and who's to know what the identity of them is?

Mr. Anderson: I am sorry, Your Honor. They're identified by source. Either a specific bank account or a specific brokerage account.

The Court: Where is that?

Mr. Anderson: I don't have a summary—(Interruption).

The Court: As to in, does any of that need to be admitted into evidence?

Mr. Anderson: I believe that is needs to be admitted into evidence so that Agent Vest can testify as to his summaries, which he has prepared, based upon those documents.

The Court: I don't know of any such rule as that, that everything that a person relies on for a summary be admitted into evidence.

Mr. Anderson: I do, Your Honor, based on Federal Rule of Evidence 1006. Its Tenth Circuit case law that it either has to be admitted by stipulation or admitted into evidence in order for the agent to rely on.

Mr. Bryant: I don't have any objection. As I understood it, they were going to use these documents a foundation for summary or summation of evidence by the case agent. I don't have any objection to them being admitted to serve as a kind of –

The Court: Well, what I'm curious about is that you want all of these exhibits marked and admitted in evidence?

Mr. Anderson: Yes, Your Honor, or by stipulation. They do not have to come into evidence. I was only doing that for the convenience of the Court. They do not have to come in if they're admitted by stipulation. The Ninth Circuit specifically says that.

The Court: Do you have any objection to that, Mr. Bryant?

Mr. Bryant: No, Your Honor.

The Court: I don't know what it is. But if you don't—do you want 1 through 11 admitted into evidence? Is that what—

Mr. Anderson: Yes, Your Honor.

The Court: You move 1 through 11? You have no objection?

Mr. Bryant: No, Sir.

The Court: Show 1 through 11 admitted without objection. Now, what else?

Mr. Anderson: Well, Your Honor, we have a stipulation which is Government Exhibit No. 80 and No. 82. If I thought

I'd raise that with the Court at this time, however, whenever it's convenient for the Court, we would like those read to the jury.

The Court: You want 80, 81, and 82 read to the jury?

Mr. Anderson: Yes, please.

The Court: You agree that 80, 81, and 82 may be admitted in evidence? That's what he asked.

Mr. Bryant: If he could identify them. I've seen some stipulations.

The Court: Why don't you come up and look at them?

Mr. Bryant: I have no objection.

The Court: Show them admitted without objection. Do you what all of this to go to the jury? Do you want the pile of material here and also 80, 81, and 82 to go to the jury?

Mr. Anderson: Your Honor, I don't believe these documents need to go to the jury.

The Court: Do you agree, Mr. Bryant? That those not go to the Jury.

Mr. Bryant: Yes, Your Honor.

(My lawyer has not only agreed to allow 70,000 documents into evidence without knowing their eventual use, he has helped them do it. The Jury has not been brought in yet, and Mr. Bryant has already screwed me and lost my case for me).

One of the Jury Members is Mrs. Michelle E. Barrett. She teaches school in Sallisaw, Oklahoma. Her Husband works for the Oklahoma Department of Transportation as a maintenance worker. I was on the Sallisaw City Counsel for six years and State Representative for six more. The town has 5,000 people do you really think she would not know me? In addition to lying to get on the jury, she and her husband are related to one of the owners. Bill Ford is on the School Board and likely was the person who hired her. My scheme to lose my money and that of my friends in the Stock Market has been exposed. This theory is so dumb its unreal.

Clearly, my constitutional rights to an impartial jury have been violated. Mr. Bryant was asked to keep anyone from Sallisaw off the jury.

"In fact, I don't think you should allow anyone from my County, on the jury." I told him. Donald Arnold was also on the jury. He is a retired Federal Government employee who said, before the trial, "They wouldn't brings him in if he wasn't guilty."

Jury pool member, Roger D. Ballard, overheard him say this. Two others repeated it more than once. Mr. Ballard is a friend of mine. He was seated on the jury and excused himself (as Mrs. Barrett should have). Juror, Mrs. Barrett, falsely claims she doesn't know me and I know why? Juror, Mr. Donald Arnold falsely claims he believes me innocent until proven guilty. Why would he say that?

The witness part of the trial has not even started, and I have two reversible errors. The Jury must be impartial and my Attorney is required to advise me of the plea offer—two reversible errors and we have not even begin presenting evidence in my illegal trial. (It is 11:30 am, when the Court finally allows Mr. Raley to make his opening statements)

Mr. Raley: Good afternoon, ladies and gentlemen. The Court has already introduced the lawyers that are involved in this trial for the next two or three days. I'm assisted by Assistant U.S. Attorney, Mr. William Anderson, of my staff, Mr. Richard Condvertiono, who is a Special Attorney with the Fraud Section of the Department of Justice in Washington, DC (He could have added and sent to us my the Honorable U.S. Senator from Oklahoma, David Lyle Boren). Also, Mr. Tom Vest. Mr. Vest is a Special Agent (they are all special agents) for the Federal Bureau of Investigation. Mr. Vest will also be called as a witness in this case. Mr. Vest will not only be introduced to you as a Special Agent of the Federal Bureau of Investigation, but as a professional accountant.

Mr. Craig Bryant, is the attorney who represents Mr. Bob O. Parris, of Sallisaw. Mr. Parris is the Defendant in this case. As the judge has advised you, Bob O. Parris of Sallisaw is charged in three separate counts. Generally speaking, those charges amount to the use of the mail to defraud. At the appropriate time, the Court will give us all of the applicable law that we will need to have in order to make a determination as to the facts in this case. At that time, I believe that the Court may describe to you the elements of mail fraud.

I'll not presume upon you or the Court at this time except to advise you that we believe that at the time that the Government has concluded the presentation of all of its testimony and exhibits, that you will conclude with us that the Defendant, Bob O. Parris, is guilty as charged in the Grand Jury indictment.

As the evidence unfolds, you will hear testimony, and have opportunity to review documentation which will show that sometime in the latter part of 1979 or early 1980 and extending up through and until sometime in the latter part of June of 1986 in the Eastern District of Oklahoma and generally in the Sallisaw, Oklahoma area.

The Defendant, Bob O. Parris, who will be described to you incidentally by a number of witnesses as a former civic leader in Sallisaw, a former State legislator, a man who had his own accounting and tax consultant business in Sallisaw, a man who over a span of time, as witnesses will describe to us, had developed a sense of confidence and trust among people in Sallisaw and the surrounding area. And that during that time span that I just described to you—that is the latter part of '79 and 1980 and up through 1986—Mr. Bob O. Parris, using that trust and that confidence, was able to convince his former clients and customers that they should invest some of their money in what he called and what was named Parris Management Trust.

A number of these investors will come and provide to you, during the next several days, their story. They will tell you of the story that he told them about investing in this trust. They will talk to you about those things that convinced them that they should part with their money, some of which amounted to lifetime savings, and invest in the Parris Management Trust. In addition to these investors, there will be representatives of certain brokerage firms. Some three separate firms with which Mr. Parris did business and with which and into which certain funds were placed and deposited. We will produce witnesses who will detail information regarding the manner in which, during this span of time, Mr. Parris converted funds held in Trust to him for his own use.

The evidence will show that during this period of time when the trust supposedly was making money—and I'll go into that in just a few moments, some of the statements that he made and the proof that we intend to produce for you consideration—but during this period of time, he purchased an airplane. He purchased a number of very expensive, greyhounds race dogs. He made home payments or made payments on mortgages on his home. He financed a Chevrolet agency. And the evidence will show during the course of this trial by witnesses that we intend to produce and primarily with the summation testimony of Special Agent Vest, that in many cases the funds used to purchase these items for his own personal use, funds that were converted to his own personal use, came directly if—or came indirectly, if not in many cases directly, from the investors who had invested their money in his program.

In the fall of 1984, as the evidence will reveal, he paid in excess of $100,000 for a new Cessna airplane at a time when the trust was losing money. We'll be able to show through the testimony of Special Agent Vest through documentation and the testimony of witnesses, the money used to purchase that $100,000 dog and that $100,000 airplane came from funds that had been commingled in the Parris Management Trust. And, he paid $200,000 for the Chevrolet Dealership and used investor funds. We will show some $440,000 plus was in his own personal account. And almost 890,000 was spent on embezzled funds. And yet, this man right here the evidence will show, Bob O. Parris, knew from the beginning that the trust was not making any money. He will — we will show that he had admitted that he was the only one to manage the trust.

We will show that he has admitted that the investor's money was turned over rely to him for management; that no one gave him any instructions how to manage the trust, but that he did it on his own; that he kept trying to catch up and got further and further behind; that he kept asking for and receiving more and more money from his victims, as they themselves will describe from the witness stand; that he kept telling them that everything was okay; that it's looking good. You're making 12-percent interest, not to worry. That it's all insured, that it's backed by the United States Government.

All of these statements, ladies and gentlemen, to the investors were calculated by this man to deceive them into thinking that their investment was good to lull them into a sense of false security. A lady now living in the nursing home will testify, invested in this man almost a million dollars, if not more. And just a few short weeks before the collapse, testimony will reflect that he went to this lady and took the last $32,000 that she had remaining.

"What a big bunch of bullshit. Can he lie like that?" I asked by Attorney.

6

(The opening statement *I would have made, if allowed*)

Mr. Parris: Ladies and gentlemen, the Government has followed me around for five years. Everything they present here today, they've had in their hands for, at least, four years ago. Had I used investor funds to pay "in excess of $100,000" for an Airplane in 1984, I got away with it. The Government knew everything it in 1986, and should have charged me before 1989. Why did they allow me to get away with it? Because I never used investor funds and $18,500 was all that was paid for the plane. The evidence will show the owners hired Sallisaw Attorney, John Cripps, to form a Trust and name it after My Grandmother (who became the trustor). The Trustee's contracted me to manage the portfolio, not do their accounting or anything else. The dog business belonging to Mrs. Parris and she in fact paid for the Dog from the more than $500,000 she received in breeding fees and a bank loan she obtained from Commercial National Bank in Muskogee, Oklahoma. The Chevy Dealership was financed with Bank loans were from the Commercial National Bank in Muskogee, Oklahoma, and GMAC provided the money to operate and maintain the car business. I will present the loan record from the Bank connecting each payment to the Contractors Invoice and Payment. The Government commingled bank accounts, interest, and insurance, in order to fabricate their illegal case against me.

Remember…all the things the Government presents here today, they have known for five years. Only one $32,000 deposit was made in 1986. That check was brought to my office without it being solicited, and remained in the Investment Companies Checking account three weeks later when I quit the Company. No Wire was used to get it. No mail or mailings were ever used to ask for people to invest in this Company. The check was made out to the Company, not to me. It was deposited *in the Company's Checking Account in Fayetteville, Arkansas, the same day it was received and not commingled in my personal business checking account in Sallisaw, Oklahoma.*

When I left the Company on May 16, 1986, there was $331,000 in the account. Like I said before, it included the deposit Mrs. Milligan had made to her investment company eighteen days earlier.

In 1989, the Government past the chance to prosecute for the purchase of the Airplane in 1984. Only $18,500 was paid it and that came out of my personal Business Checking Account in Sallisaw, Oklahoma. No matter, it is just too late, sorry. When the Government goes around harassing a person for five years before asking for an indictment, it is past the limit of time allowed by law for them to file charges. It's sort of like they make you suffer for five years, then ask the Courts to punish you for another five or more. It's against the law for a good reason and it's not fair for them to abuse their power like this.

We will present a one million-dollar fidelity insurance policy and call the salesman to prove it has a rider for "Investment Advisor" (which is what I was for this investment company—not the owner—or,—the Accountant).

The owners filed court action on June 3, 1986. Their Attorney, Jim Jones, knew about the Insurance, but no claim has ever been filed. This is because the owners found out the $300,000 they claimed I diverted to my personal use, never happened. The Government now tells you "almost $890,000 was spent from investor's funds." Why not say 7.9 million or 16.8? Going from $300,000 to $890,000 doesn't seem like enough of an increase. If they are going to lie, why not make it a good one.

Commingling funds, false pretense, mailing two checks, telling a lady, over the phone, that I have Insurance. Needing the $32,000 so bad that I twisted the poor woman's arm — then, never used it. What kind of criminal am I anyway? In the indictment, the Government has alternated from the Company's checking account being in Sallisaw and calling it commingling of funds; too, it being in Fayetteville, in order for me to mail the check somewhere. They called the IRS Tax Code "false Pretense"—85% tax free income between Corporation's, and capital gains being 50% Tax-free. They laugh at someone offering to find investments in the stock market paying 12%. Today getting 12% interest is only for the credit card companies, but in 1980, it was below the prime rate. The owners invested in their Company, not in me. Mr. Bill Ford was the Trustee in charge of the Accounting, not me.

In June of 1980, the evidence will show, I was contracted to manage the portfolio and invest in stock paying 12%. Not how much the Investment Company would make, or, their beneficial shares would be worth. That would be the business of the Trustee's not me.

In 1978, my family and I formed a personal business corporation and called it Parris Management Service. The Government will confuse and abuse the rule of law by making this personal family business checking account appear to be the same as Parris Management Trust which was formed in June of 1980. In addition to the Government commingling the Checking Accounts they group together three kinds of Interest: Beneficial Interest in the Trust, Interest paid or received on money invested, and Applied Interest.

A Trust is taxes by the IRS as a Corporation and ownership is denoted as the amount of Beneficial Interest you own in the Trust. Interest received by this Investment Company from another Corporation is called dividends, and they are 85% tax-free. A person holding beneficial interest (shares) in a trust for more than 12 months are eligible to treat the profit as a capital gain (in 1980 a capital gain is 50% tax free). The Company had two kinds of Insurance. Insurance against theft of investment's, and insurance on money in the checking or savings account. There is no Insurance against Stocks going up or down. The Government has commingled the Parris Management Service (a family held corporation) with Parris Management Trust (a public trust) And, alleged true statements in the IRS Code are false pretense. Neither of the two check's the Government claims I mailed were from me, or, too me. Evidence will show I did not mail the $32,000 check. The $800.00 Company check mailed on May 20th, three days after I was gone.

On June 17, 1986, a month after I was no longer with the investment company, and two weeks after a lawsuit had been filed against me, by the owners, I answered the phone (count

II) in order to "lull" the caller into not filing the court action she had already filed on June 3, 1986. We are not taking about reasonable doubt in this case. We are talking about clear and convincing evidence that there was no case in 1988, when U.S. Attorney Roger Hilfinger declared, after a three year investigation: "The investigation is complete and we are not going to seek an indictment." It is clear why the former U.S. Attorney, Roger Hilfinger, never filed for an indictment. There was no case then and there sure is no case now.

Take away the false documents used by the new U.S. Attorney, John Raley, and the lies told by special FBI Agent, Tom Vest, and you find twelve people who tragically lost a lot of money in the Stock Market. If finding me guilty would return their money and mine, we would not be here today. I would do almost anything to get the money back, including pleading guilty to intentionally losing my money and that of my friends in the stock market.

I lost $350,000 in my personal business hoping I would make enough money to replace the loss my friends and family had. Had it not been for the FBI following me around for the past five years, affecting my wife's Greyhound Business, she would be making money today. Bill Ford slipped up on me and sucker punched in the barbershop, we are even. If the other owners want to hit me a couple of times for being stupid, that might also be justified. I think that is enough punishment for losing money in the Stock Market.

(Instead of the above, The following was My Defense:)

Mr. Bryant: Ladies and Gentlemen of the Jury make the government prove their case against Mr. Parris beyond a reasonable doubt. They have the burden of proof.

After Bryant's very extra short brief opening statement, the Judge read the following: Government's Exhibit 80. It is hereby stipulated by and between the parties that Government's Exhibit

Nos. 54 and 55, copies of deposition transcripts of Defendant, Bob O. Parris, taken June 25th, 1986 and September 9th, 1986, respectfully, are true and correct transcriptions of the testimony rendered by Bob O. Parris on the subject date.

No. 81 is stipulation by the parties as to the admissibility of banking and financial records. And, it goes this way: In order to preserve judicial time and resources and to simplify the trial of this matter to the greatest extent possible, the parties hereby stipulate to the admissibility into evidence at trial of any and all of the following prescribed banking and financial records. (The Court entered 70,000 documents dating from 1968 through 1988)

In Exhibit Number 82: It is hereby stipulated by the parties—(the Court enters all of my Wife's, her dad's, and nineteen other people's greyhound transfers—two thousand transfers over a nine-year period. The ONE greyhound actually being mine had a total value of Three Hundred Dollars).

7

The Court: Call your first witness.

Mr. Condvertiono: Your Honor, the United States calls Bill Ford. Whereupon, the witness was sworn.

(Only the important testimony has been reprinted here. It is recorded just as it is in the transcript (errors and all). The complete testimony of all, or any, of the witnesses may be obtained by writing the author.)

DIRECT EXAMINATION

Q Was the trust to be insured, sir?

A My understanding it was, yes.

Q How did you reach that understanding?

A He told me that he had an accounting bond.

Q Mr. Ford, you just said he told you?

A   Bob. Bob Parris told me that had—he was bonded through an accounting office and that the investment was insured, as safe as the U.S. Government.

Q   Did you rely on that?

A   Yes, I did.

Q   Now, I want to bring you back to early 1980 about the initial investment. Do you recall how much you first invested with Mr. Parris?

"Are you going to object?" I asked my lawyer.

"Why?" he asks.

"Well for one thing, he never invested with me or in me. He is one of the owners, and I am the portfolio manager. The jury should know that right off the bat, don't you think?" I said.

A   I invested $60,000 the first time.

Q   Now, did there come a time when you invested more money with Mr. Parris, sir?

A   Yes, sir, there was.

Q   Can you tell us when that was

A   '84

Q   in '84, how much did you invest with Mr. Parris?

A   Three hundred and 10,000.

Q   Did there come a time, Mr. Ford, when you began to get concerned about your investment?

A   Yes, sir there was.

Q   —of 370,000? Can you tell us when that was?

A   '84.

Q   Have you recovered any of it?

A   Some.

CROSS EXAMINATION

Mr. Bryant rambled around asking the same question the Washington fraud lawyer asked. Nothing important was coming out. I got my lawyer over to the table and said. *"You ask him how much 'some' is. And if he ever had an audit performed.*

Or, I'm going to jail for attacking your sorry ass right here in this Courtroom."

Q How long were you chairman of the Trust?

A From the time it started till we disbanded it.

Q Has the Trust been dissolved?

A It's in the process of being dissolved.

Q When was Bob Parris hired as manager of the trust?

A When we got the corporate papers fixed up and ready.

Q That was back in 1980, not 1979?

A When it was formed in June 1980.

Q How long did he continue as manager of the trust?

A May the 16th, 1986.

Q In hiring Mr. Parris as manager, did you all give him powers to invest your money?

A Yes.

Q You testified that you put some money in 1980 and some more in 1984, did you make any withdrawals from the trust?

A There was a little bit. Probably—I don't remember just what it was, but there was very little....—

Q How much?

A —if any. I don't have any idea, you know, on the withdrawals.

Q You say a little amount?

A On the 60, I don't believe I withdrew anything on the 60,000.

Q Then, you said you made a second investment in 1984. Did you make any withdrawals after the....

A After 1984?

Q Yes, sir.

A There was two withdrawals, yes.

Q First withdrawal, what was the amount of that?

A Well, the first withdrawal was 90,000 to clear my corporate notes and everything.

Q How did you get that $90,000?

A Bob wrote me a check for it.

Q Wrote it on the trust account in Fayetteville?

A Yes.

Q And the second withdrawal, what was the amount of that withdrawal?

A One Hundred and 25,000

Q When was that made?

A Just before the trust effectively had collapsed.

Q The Trust collapsed on May 16, 1986, when was this check written?

A May 16, 1986.

Q Sure it was for Hundred and 25,000?

A Could have been another 160,000 or so.

Q Did you and the Trustee's file a lawsuit against Mr. Parris?

A Yes.

Q You were one of the Plaintiffs in that lawsuit?

A Yes, sir.

Q As a trustee of this trust, do you recall whether you all had assumed the duty to have an audit performed of the trust every year?

A Yes.

Q Was an audit ever done?

A No.

Q Never done from '80-'86?

A No, there wasn't.

REDIRECT EXAMINATION

By Mr. Condvertiono:

Q Mr. Ford, you were cut off a couple of times and I want to ask you about particularly the accounting bond. Do you recall…

A Yes.

Q —being asked about the accounting bond? Were you ever contacted by a representative of a bonding company in order to reimburse you for the amount lost?

A No, sir, I wasn't

Jim Harrell Lee became the next witness. He invested $40,000 in the trust and had not removed any money. This was the owner I wanted the Insurance Policy handed too. The Government asked him if anyone had contacted him from any insurance or bonding company. Of course, the owners failed to file a claim. So, Why would the Insurance Company contact them?

The Court: We'll recess until 1:50 p.m.

J.O. Farmer was the first witness after lunch.

DIRECT EXAMINATION

By Mr. Anderson

J.O. Farmer and the others trusted me to make money and I let them down, no argument about that. Mr. Farmer told the Court he put in $100,000 and took out $6,000. I told Mr. Bryant he was withdrawing $675.00 per month. He put in a total of $72,500 and removed $18,250. J.O. Admitted he was taking out $675.00 a month to pay for an uncle he had in the nursing home. He also took out another $3,000 when his son died. Mr. Farmer actually lost $52,000 in the trust. I asked my Attorney to show him the One Million-Dollar Insurance Policy.

"I'm tired of them asking these witnesses if they knew anything about a bond or insurance."

Mr. Bryant refused.

Eldon Rambin, the A.G. Edwards & sons stockbroker was called as the Government's next witness against me. He admitted as a stockbroker he carried insurance, and his company also carried insurance. "Mr. Parris bought and sold stock". What else could he testify about? It was in 1980, 81, 82, and '83, so, why we were discussing it. After all, I could have stole the entire amount and the Government would have waited to long to do anything about it in 1991.

Bill Ford's brother in law, Robert E. Suttle, was called next. He put in $30,000 and Mr. Ford had not shared any of the final money with him. Like all the other owners, he trusted me to make money and I failed him. Then, the insurance thing again.

"You have to produce the insurance." I said to Mr. Bryant, for the ninth time in the past hour and five minutes.

My cousin, Billy Ed Brooks was called. He lost money. He trusted me to make money and I failed. The only thing different about his testimony was that Mr. Bryant forgot he was suppose to be helping the Government get me convicted and asked: "Do you think Mr. Parris lost money in this trust?" Mr. Brooks answered:

"Yes, I believe he did."

Gerald and Jean Ware were called. The insurance for dishonesty is beginning to sound more like insurance against losing money in the stock market.

"The Jury is going to get the wrong idea about this insurance, if you don't present it now." I told Mr. Bryant. All the owners knew they were investing in the Stock Market and what the risks were. We purchased preferred stock for the long term and that is how we were safer that the regular market. You know the amount of interest you will earn and the amount you will receive when the stock matures. That kind of talk and assurances was back in 1981, '82, and '83. From 1984 the guarantees on how much I could get on the stock I purchased for them came down to 10% in 1985, and none in 1986. The Wear's are the first witnesses to talk about 1986.

She received the $800.00 company check. It was mailed on May 20, 1986. She had not seen who mailed the check. She and the other owners filed civil action on June 3, 1986. Mrs. Ware called me on June 17, 1986, to find out about her money, if she wins the court action.

"Should we win, how will you pay?" she asked.

"I have Insurance, but you can't win because I never diverted any money to my personal use." I answered.

All I need to eliminate the wire fraud count is the Insurance policy and I ask Mr. Bryant about it about every ten minutes. I'm really worried about this entire thing. I had mailed Mrs. Ware a check for $800.00 every month for two years. I could have pled guilty to mailing a check, but where is the pattern of criminal activity? It was a company check and it was good. The check was just mailed, nothing else. Mrs. Ware confirmed the checking account for the Investment Company is a Cash Management checking Account with Merrill Lynch in Fayetteville, Arkansas, but no one pointed out the Government's deception to the Court or Jury. The Insurance Company told me they would be getting in touch with the owners within the next couple of weeks. That is what I told everyone. They never showed up because they were never included in the court action. I wonder if my wife, mother, and Cousin could re-open the case against me in Civil Court, add the Insurance Company as a codefendant in the action and get their money back. The Government has proven their case for them.

8

The Government 2 million dollars had been invested in the Investment Company over a six-year period, from July 1, 1980 through June 12, 1987. You might think this is longer than six years, but you have to realize this, after all, is our Government and show some respect. One million 700,000 was the correct amount and from July 1, 1980 through May 16, 1986, was the correct time period. Early in May, I had asked Special Agent Vest to make me a copy of his accounting register. I knew the first time we looked at the seven boxes full of papers. Agent Vest overstated the investments in the Company. At the close of trial on the first day (June 3rd), Vest handed me a copy of that report and said he was going to use it the next day when he testified. I found where he posted almost $265,000 in other Companies. These investments that belonged to investments of individuals in there own personal stockbroker's account, and had nothing to do with the Company where I managed the portfolio.

I was fairly certain when I proved the fact I never used any of the owner's funds, or gained in any way from this Investment Company's bad luck; the case could be over.

It was late when I called U.S. Senator BOREN'S personal private secretary in Washington, DC. Pam Dobbler had been BOREN'S Secretary since he was in the Oklahoma House of Representative in 1970. I knew her to be one of the most honest and reliable people in the world. She wouldn't lie to me, even to save Boren's ass.

"Pam, I am worried that David is still after me."

"Why do you think that?" She asked.

"A special fraud Attorney from the Justice Department in Washington is down here hammering at me."

"You and David buried the hatchet several years ago."

"I know, but Bill Ford is going all over town telling everyone 'he called Senator Boren' and told him this was the last chance he had to get the guy who pulled the flag down. Four days after he begin saying that, I got the indictment notice."

"David got really mad at you about that." Pam said.

"He did a good job of keeping me from getting re-elected and he got my dad fired that should be enough."

"I know he has made a few calls to keep you from getting a job, but that's all. David would never go this far, unless he thinks you're guilty and getting away with something." She said.

"I'm really worried, my lawyer ain't gonna to do anything, so, I'm likely to look guilty. If I had all this money they claim I stole, I could hire Bruce Green or Gene Stipe and get off. David can do a lot with judge Seay because they are both from Seminole, Oklahoma, and David got President Carter to appointed him to the Federal Bench. This is becoming a total nightmare, not just for me, but for my family as well. My lawyer is doing nothing and the Government is lying all over the place. Please, Pam, do what you can, I never imagined my action's as a House Member would cost me my freedom." I said

"I'll check around and let you know, I hope everything works out, you were the most honest guy up there in Oklahoma City. If you would have been quite on that darn Water Bill, he would have appointed you to anything and helped you do whatever you wanted." Pam said.

I said, "Even a judgeship. I could go back to school a couple of years and become a Federal Judge. Just think I could be the Judge and Frank Howell Seay could be the criminal, if it weren't so sad it would be funny, Thanks Pam, see you later."

"Did you know, not getting the water bill passed cost David a $300,000 dollar contribution from an engineering firm in Oklahoma City? They were going to do the 3 million dollar study for the Corps of Engineers?" Pam asked

"My God, no wonder he got so mad. No, I never knew that. Did you know a couple of boys wanted to expose David during his first U.S. Senate race?"

I woke up at 3 a.m. in a cold sweat and almost didn't make it to the pot. I was really sick, but I wanted this trial over and I knew VEST'S errors would end the case.

Court convened for the second day with me having to go get a shot for chest pains and diarrhea. The clinic gave me a shot of Demerol and Levison.

I sat in Mr. Bryant's office the better part three hours before feeling like I was regaining control. Before going to the Doctor, I handed my Attorney a copy of Vest's five or six page statement with marks on the A.G. Edwards & Sons account numbers Agent Vest had misused.

"The total amount invested over the six year period was One million $700,000. $900,000 had been returned during that period. And, at the end Mr. Ford received $331,000 I say he got, or, $260,000 Mr. Ford says he received. The Company lost $600,000 in the Stock Market." I said. It had been my understanding that we were going to discuss some of the questions my lawyer should be asking instead of him asking the same ones the Government asked.

As we set down at the defense table, in the Courtroom, Special Agent Vest handed me a one-page, nine-line statement headed *Victim's* Investments in Parris' Scheme (exhibit 99). The $300,000 dollars in errors had not been corrected. Shockingly, the new report actually increased the amount invested in the Company over the six-year period from 2 million to 2.5 million. Now, Special Agent Vest's lying has increased another $500,000. Agent Vest claims $2.5 million was invested and "Parris diverted over $889,008 to his personal use."

I asked Mr. Bryant, "What did you have to do with this, where is the printout I gave you, you will need that copy to impeach this fabricated garbage. After a five-year investigation they overstated the amount Invested by $300,000. Within one hour after you showed them their error they found another $500,000 had actually been invested."

"We will present our case after the government gets finished." Bryant said.

I said, "You and I know the case will be over if you don't clear up some of these lies as we go along. Hell, it probably already too late. With the idiot mistakes you have already made.

The second line claims Investor's put securities in the Company. Do you see that? Brokerages Firms want allow this to happen. If you brought 500 shares of stock into Merrill Lynch and wanted it to go into some other account, Merrill Lynch would have to sell the stock first, then deposit the money from the sale, not the Stock. Agent Vest knew this and he knows I know it, He can only expect to get away with it

because he has you, babe." I told my crooked Appointed
Lawyer.

"You will keep still and leave the Defense to me." Mr.
Bryant replied.

(Of course, you have guessed by now that nothing was presented for the Defense).

**DIRECT EXAMINATION OF JOSEPHINE W. MILLI-
GAN.**

By Mr. Raley:

Q Over what span of time? That is, over how many years
did you and he discuss the trust and deal together on that
trust, do you know?

A I would say six years

Q And during that six years, do you have any idea how
much money you invested with him?

A One Million $800,000.

Q Tell us what you have in your hand that's marked
Government's Exhibit 23, please?

A I gave him a check for $32,000.

Q Would you read to the record the date that's on that
check?

A 4-29-86.

Q What did you do with that check?

A I gave it to Mr. Parris.

Q And, on what date did you give it to him?

A This date, 4-29-86.

Mr. Bryant established the fact that the mail was never used
between us. Of course, Mrs. Milligan's mental condition never
allowed for her to be a competent witness. The Government
was giving lip service to Mrs. Milligan's investment in the
company being in the neighborhood of a million dollars. They
knew she put in and took out three hundred thousand twice.

A million 800,000 was more than everyone put in the company.

"Ask her to look on the back of the check and tell us what date Merrill Lynch deposited it." I said (Merrill Lynch deposited the check on 4-29-86).

"She is to demented." Bryant said

9

DIRECT EXAMINATION OF GERALD TOMLINSON

By Mr. Condvertiono (the Washington, DC Lawyer)

Q Where do you work?

A Merrill Lynch.

Q And, how long have you know Mr. Parris?

A Since 1978. Going on 13 years.

Mr. Condvertiono: I would like to show if I may, Your Honor, what's already been admitted Government Exhibit 23. I would like to show that to the witness, if I may sir.

The Court: All right.

Q You have before you a check, is that right?

A Yes.

Q Will you tell us who signed that check? Do you see that name?

A Yes.

Q Will you tell us who signed that check? Do you see that name?

A Josephine Milligan.

Q And, the amount of that check, sir?

A Thirty two thousand.

Q And, the date?

A 4-29-86

Q And, who is the check made out to?

A Parris Management Trust.

Q Now, if you'll turn the check over, please. Is there anything on the back that would indicate Merrill Lynch received this check?

A That was deposited to our bank in Fayetteville, Arkansas.

Q Was this check mailed to Merrill Lynch in Fayetteville?

A Yes.

Q How do you know that

A Virtually all of our business is transacted through the mail.

"Ask him what the name of the Merrill Lynch employee he sent down to purchase a Vehicle from me, in Sallisaw on 4-29-86. We subpoena that guy and he will testify that he hand carried the $32,000 check back with him and gave it to the Merrill Lynch cashier the same day. Ask him if the date on the back shows the date of the deposit."

CROSS EXAMINATION

By Craig Bryant:

Q Did you ever have occasion to go to Sallisaw to attend a meeting of the trustees?

A Yes.

Q Do the Trustees call you to ask how the things are going?

A Only Bill Ford.

Q Did you tell him?

A Yes

Q You had no probation from tell any of the Owners whatever they wanted to know, did you?

A No

Q When was this account established?

A March of '84.

Q Did the account just lose money?

A No, it went up and down.

Q Is Merrill Lynch cover by Insurance?

A Yes.

Q The check that you testified about, I believe it's exhibit No. 23, did you happen to see the envelope this check came in?

A I don't recall. I—I don't know.

Q You don't recall seeing it?

A No, I don't.

Q Is the mail actually opened by someone other than yourself?

A By the cashiers.

Q You don't have the envelope the check came in?

A No

Q Have you made any effort to look for it?

A No. We don't save envelopes for six years.

Q Mr. Tomlinson, you don't know for certain that particular check was delivered in the mail, do you?

A I can be awful close to certain.

Mr. Bryant: No more Questions.

"You never asked him what the name of the guy who picked up the Chevy blazer on April 29, 1986. Or, the date on the back of the check."

"Shut up and set still." He said.

I said, "You are by far the sorriest lawyer in the world!"

Mr. Condvertiono on redirect:

Q Tell us: this account, what was the overall loss?

A Around $197,000.

Q Sir, any doubt in you mind how this check arrived in Fayetteville, Arkansas on *4-29-86?*

A No.

The Federal U.S. Lawyer from Washington is admitting the Check arrived in Arkansas the same day it was written (4-29-86). The Federal U.S. mail is not that fast, from Sallisaw to Fayetteville is two days.

The other stockbroker set the first three years loss at $400,000. We now know from this broker, the loss for the last two and a half years is $197,000. The trust actually made money in 1986. Before May 16, 1986 is all the Government can charge me for. Whatever Bill Ford lost after that time is his responsibility, not mine.

The only Government witness that testified about the mailing of the $32,000 was a salesman who never went to the mailroom. The Merrill Lynch employee who hand carried the check from Sallisaw to Fayetteville was not named or called to testify on my behalf.

Mary Merrill was next to testify. She beat the IRS out of $500 by borrowing $2,000 and putting it in an IRA Account. When she got her refund, with the extra $500, she was required to lower the 2,000 loan by the $500. The Government lost $500, but poor Mrs. Merrill never lost a dime. Here she is, ranting on the witness stand about how much I displaced her.

Anthony Puglisi was called to testify. He sold me his Greyhound Booking at the Tampa Track for $50,000. I paid Carol a commission of 35% for running her dogs at the Tampa Track, in Florida. The amount was to be paid from the Greyhound's winnings at the track. Mr. Puglisi could not get good dogs, so; he made a deal with someone who could. That summer Carol's dogs won $178,000 and Anthony Puglisi paid me $128,000 and I paid Carol $62,300. It cost me $23,000 for two trainers and $14,008 for supplies. I made a little. This was in 1987, and had nothing to do with anything in 1986. Federal U.S. Pubic Defender, Mr. Bryant, and Federal U.S. Attorney, Mr. Raley, made a masterful effort in there attempt to prove I paid him $50,000 from Investor Funds, and keep the jury from knowing about the $128,000 income. Mr. Puglisi managed to tell the jury without being asked. Thank you Tony!

Edwin A. Craig was the next witness called by the Government. Mr. Craig sold my Wife, Carol, and a Greyhound for the bargain price of $100,000. I say bargain because the stud fee for the dog was $1,500 and he was bred over 600 times according to Carol and National Greyhound Records (where every breeding must be filed). The Dog was bred a hundred and forty-eight times in 1984 and 85 (i.e. during the time Carol was making payments on the dog). Kunta Kinta was the Dog's name. We called him Toby. His litter was named after the characters in "*Roots*."

Kunta Kinta (Toby) is a member of the Greyhound hall of fame in Abilene, Kansas. Carol owes all her success, in the dog business, to this great dog, and getting Tim and Cindy Cahill to train and run her dogs, at the track. The Government wants to use the cost of the dog Carol purchased, but not the loan she made to purchase him, or, the $500,000 in revenue from his stud service. And, of course the U.S. Public Defender, Mr. Bryant would never break his agreement with the U.S. Attorney, John Raley, and bring these facts out.

10

DIRECT EXAMINATION OF EDWIN A. CRAIG

By Mr. Raley:

Q I'll ask you if you know the defendant in this case?

A Yes, he is right over there.

Q Have you ever met him before?

A Yes, one time.

Q When was that?

A September the 10th, 1984.

Q Is there some particular reason why you remember that exact date?

A It's my birthday anniversary.

Q For what purpose was the contact?

A I delivered a greyhound.

Q Who was present when you delivered the dog?

A Carol Parris and Bob Parris.

Q Were you ever paid for this dog?

A Yes, sir.

Q How was you paid for the dog?

A I received $50,000 down and $10,000 per month for the next five months. If the dog remained sound for breeding during that period. No refunds.

Q Were you paid?

A Yes.

My Lawyer on cross—(Unbelievable)

By Mr. Bryant:

Q Mr. Craig, do you know why Bob Parris was purchasing this dog?

A Sir, I am hard of hearing, so just—okay, give me that again.

Q Do you know why Bob Parris purchased this dog?

A Did Bob Parris purchase it?

Q Why did he purchase it?

A I have no idea.

Q Do you know whether he purchased it for breeding purposes?

A I assume that's what he did.

Q Is there money to be made from breeding greyhounds?

A Yes, sir. I could understand the other attorney, but—just slow up a little.

Mr. Bryant: I apologize. I you—(Interruption)

The Court: You will do much better, I think, if you just stand away from the microphone. Completely away from it, probably, so that your voice doesn't come over.

Q How's this, Mr. Craig? Is this better?

A Yeah.

Q He didn't give you a check for $100,000 when he took possession of the dog, did he?

A You're saying he?

Q Mr. Parris.

A Sir, this is seven years ago. I don't know who made those checks out.

Q You didn't get a check for $100,000 from Bob Parris?

A I didn't—not 100,000. I got one for $50,000 and the rest were paid in, I think, 10,000 payments until the $100,000 was paid. Then I signed the greyhound over to Carol Parris.

Q Signed it over to Carol Parris not to Bob Parris?

A Uh-huh.

Q As best you can remember, it took approximately six months for Mr. Parris to pay you off?

A Now, you say Mr. Parris? I don't remember who signed the check.

Q Whoever received the checks took six months?

A Sir, I can't—can that man come up here?

The Court: I think you need to speak up. Just stand to your left and then speak up. You drop parts of words and parts of your sentence.

Mr. Bryant: I'm *sorry,* no more questions.

Have you ever heard the expression—"did he help me out?" and the comic guy says—"Yeah, he helped me plumb out." I'm glad Bryant admitted to being sorry. At least, he got that right. Lawyers are sometime inept and brain deficient, but Mr. Bryant is the first out and out crooked lawyer I've met up close and personal. He tries to prove I bought the $100,000 dog for the Government. Bryant knew Carol received a loan for $50,000 to make the down payment, and bred the dog seven to twelve time a month at $1,500 dollars a pop. During the 12 months after the purchase, Carol received in over $150,000. She repaid the loan and made the monthly payment at the same time. She was also able to put money in our personal business checking account in Sallisaw, Oklahoma, to pay the electric bills and mortgage payments.

Carol could have removed $50,000 from the Investment Company any time. She put in $30,000 and mom would have loaned her up to $50,000 more. Carol could have removed it, or I could have removed it for her before I turned the portfolio management Job over the Mr. Ford.

There should be a law requiring lawyers like Craig Bryant and John Raley to be put in prison for intentionally ruining people's lives like this. Special Agents, who are dishonest, like Tom Vest, should have a really special place in the bottom of an outdoor toilet.

The next to last witness is the person who sold me the alleged $100,000 airplane. Problem is, I only paid $18,500 for the plane.

DIRECT EXAMINATION OF WILLIAM CHRISTIANSEN

By Mr. Raley:

Q Have you ever done business with Mr. Parris?

A Yes, I sold him a Cessna single engine airplane.

Q Tell us the amount—the full amount of the purchase price?

A I believe it was $108,500.

Q Do you recall the nature of the manner in which this $108,500 was paid?

A I believe he paid $18,500 down and financed $90,000.

Q What eventually happened to the airplane?

A It is my understanding that it burned in a hanger fire in Sallisaw.

The Government, Agent Vest, and Mr. Bryant are well aware of the fact that only $18.500 was paid for the Airplane. Intentionally misleading the jury on material facts, to gain a Conviction, Is illegal and criminal.

The Government knowingly lied to the jury: (1) $100,000 of investor funds being used to purchase the Airplane. (2)

$100,000 of investor funds was used to purchase a dog. (3) $200,000 of investor funds were used to purchase a chevy dealership. (4) The owners of the trust were "Victims of Parris' scheme to intentionally lose money in the stock market." (5). Parris needed these "Old Cash Cows" to pay for "Plane's", "Dogs", and "Chevy Dealerships." (6) $889,008 of investor funds was diverted to Mr. Parris' Personal use." And, (7) *Securities* from victims to Parris for Investments $498,942.46 (The law requires Securities be sold and cash invested). How many people are in prison because of a dishonest Federal Public Defenders and Special Agent for the FBI, and over zealous US Attorneys?

11

DIRECT EXAMINATION OF THOMAS VEST

By Mr. Condvertiono:

You're talking now about documents you received from whom, sir

A The *Victims.*

Q Were any documents acquired under a subpoena?

A Yes, they were.

Q What documents were those?

A Records I received from financial institutions, mainly. I received them and analyzed them, and looking for the financial transactions. Again, attempting to trace the *victims'* funds through these accounts.

Q Did you create summary report, Mr. Vest.

A Yes, I did.

Q Were you able to tell how much money the *victims* gave Mr. Parris? Tell us first before we look at that summary. You complied that summary from what information?

A From all the information I collected through my six year investigation of Mr. Parris.

Q I would like to ask you to review—have you before you document—Government Exhibit 99. Can you briefly describe what that document summarizes?

A Yes. This document traces the investor' moneys that— and securities that—with Bob Parris, beginning with the amounts that—through the period from 1980 through 1987.

The Court: Now, do you have any objection?

Mr. Bryant: No, Your Honor.

The Court: Show them admitted without objection.

Mr. Condvertiono: At this time, Your Honor, I would respectfully request that the jury be allowed to follow Mr. Vest's testimony by issuing Exhibit 99 to the for view when he testifies.

The Court: I presume you have a blowup; is that what you—

Mr. Condvertiono: Sir, we have copies for each juror.

The Court: All right.

Q Will you take us through line-by-line on this document and tell us what your calculations were?

A Yes. The first line, money from *victims* to Parris.

Q Excuse me, Mr. Vest. From herein when we see that word *victims*, would you please refer to—

The Court: Well, that doesn't make any difference. Just so you have it there. Evidently, he's seen it before today many, many, many times and didn't object to it, so just—there's no problem. Go ahead.

(In my mind I have objected every time anyone said Victims. I am of the opinion that I am innocent until proven guilty and it's up to the jury to decide. I have never had anyone call themselves Victims of me, before this trial. Thanks to my sick lawyer, the Court has just made that decision for them. "Many" was said many time too many. Definitely more than the Honorable Frank Howell Seay needed to say it. Another odd thing happened later, when I read the transcript of the trial it only had many on their once. Which is still one to many time.)

The Special Agent went on to tell the jury this was a "Classic Ponzi Scheme" and that I diverted $889,008 to my personal use. He knew he was lying about finding checks written out of investor funds for the Airplane, dog, chevy dealership. Mr. Bryant intentionally failed to use the two bank loans of $200,000 and $50,000, to prove the government was lying. Special Agent Vest knew these loans existed.

He knew he could lie and not be caught, because Mr. Bryant was in on the Scheme to convict me.

The $500,000 Income from breeding the dog was not used. The $325,000 income from Carol's race dogs was ignored, the same way they commingled by personal business checking account with the Investor's checking account. And, the same way they commingled other company's deposits and ignored the withdrawals and ending balances. If Carol took in $283,000 and deposited it in our personal business checking account, Special Agent Vest would ignore it. But, if a check for $50,000 was written to pay for the dog, he counted that as being from Investor Funds. When carol deposited $50,000 from the loan, Vest simply ignored it, or, found a way for it to be deposited by a Victim. Forget the fact that no investor's were making any investments during that time. In fact they were withdrawing money the last half of 1984.

(Keeping his job must depend on getting this conviction).

We have to keep a supply of fresh meat going into the Federal Prison System, or, lose some of their Appropriation's from the Taxpayers money.

How would you like to have a job that ruined innocent lives?

The checks from Parris Chevrolet Co., in Sallisaw, paid for the Chevy Dealership. VEST used the checks paid out for the dealership as being from the investor funds. Then, the crooked FBI guy maliciously and criminally, ignored the $200,000 loan from the Commercial National Bank. The withdrawals from the bank loan in Muskogee tied in exactly with the deposits in checking account. Clearly, the Owners of the Company made no deposits during this period for me to use and the beginning and ending balances remained the same.

As an accountant VEST would starve. There aren't many calls for a lying accountant. But, It would appear the FBI has a need for a person with this type of mentality, to keep expanding the Prison System.

"I don't want to testify." I said, as I was leaving the Courthouse at the end of the second day. I am being railroaded down the tracks to prison, and nothing I can say will make a difference.

My mind is whirling as I driving the sixty miles from Muskogee to Sallisaw. Can you believe Mr. Raley asked Agent Vest—how much money did Mr. Parris tell you he made during this period of time?

"Around $50,000." Vest replied.

He bought all this stuff on $50,000 a year is that what he wanted you to believe? Raley asked.

"Exactly." Vest answered.

Are these people for real? Every Honest person in America will tell you A self-employed person may take in $750,000 and pays out $700,000. He makes $50,000. He could have paid $18,500 for an airplane, $600,000 for a bunch of other things, and still have more than $50,000 to make the house payment and pay the utility bills. VEST and RALEY can find Carol's expense, but not her income. Find the Chevy Dealership's expense, but not it's revenue. Find four other Investment Companies Deposits and add those to this Investment Company, but they cannot find the balance remaining in those four Accounts or the amount removed by those other people from their Company. Time and time again the Government and My Attorney lied to the Court and mislead the Jury. Mr. Raley has a 98% conviction rate - Guilty or Not. It only matters that they were convicted, not their guilt or innocence. 79% of the 2% Mr. Raley lost were really guilty, they just have enough money to get a qualified attorney and escape our system of justice. There are very few rich, innocent, people in prison, and there are very few rich, guilty, people behind the razor wire of any prison in America.

Several hundred poor innocent people are suffering a fate worse than death. There is no DNA or anything like that to get them out like there is on death row. I think I am experienced enough to be able to talk to a prisoner who has been behind bars a while and know if he is innocent or not. They perspire, smell, and agonize, different than a guilty man doing the crime and doing the time.

The *Tulsa World* had big headlines on the front page the next morning:

EX-LAWMAKER OPERATED PONZI SCHEME. By: Jerry Fink.

Jury told Former State Rep. Bob Parris, D-Sallisaw, operated a "classic Ponzi Scheme" in bilking investors out of $1.8 million, an FBI agent testified Tuesday. In a Ponzi Scheme, said agent Thomas Vest, a con man solicits investors and pays them interest on their investments over a period of time using their own money or money from other investors. "The investors left in the end lose," said Vest At the conclusion of Vest's testimony, U.S. Attorney John Raley rested his case against Parris. Agent Vest told the jury Mr. Parris routinely deposited checks from investors in his business account, instead of in the trust account. "During the period the trust was operating, $2.5 million were invested and almost $1.8 million of that was lost either through bad investments or spent by Parris for his personal use." Vest said. "Money meant for the trust was used to pay Parris' utilities, medical among other personal items. Parris also built a car dealership north of Sallisaw. Parris spent $100,000 on a greyhound-racing dog and $60,000 on a kennel, noted Vest.

I quit reading and put the paper down. Listening to the lies in Court was enough.

"That story is about as close as a newspaper can get to what Agent Vest said." I told myself. Jerry Fink misquoted the FBI Agent's in a couple of spots, and failed to mention the $100,000 Airplane. Fink must have made a mistake and called the Airplane Salesman. I wish he had also called Mr. Puglisi. He could have left out the $60,000 kennel purchase. Fink must have missed some testimony, at least, the part where Mr. Puglisi received $178,000 from the Tampa Greyhound Track, withheld the purchase price, and paid me the balance. A reasonable person might think the Tampa Track paid Mr. Puglisi, not the investor's. Fink must *not* have been in the Courtroom when Mr. Craig's testimony was presented to the jury. When you don't have a lawyer, misinformation will scatter the facts into the wind and innocent people get raped in the name of sensationalism.

Later, When the Government is forced to admit Agent Vest and others committed perjury, and there was actually no Ponzi Scheme involved in this case, I found there was nothing about it in the Newspaper. Mr. Fink must have been too busy to print the facts or the truth.

12

The final day of the inquisition

I just wanted to get what they were doing to me over with. I sure believed it would be a mistake for me to testify. I could only imagine what illegal things those three lawyers for the Government would to do to me without a lawyer, or a Judge, to stop them.

I answered questions and argued my case at the same time (nothing could be worse). I admitted I lost the Investor's money in the stock market.

Why did I say that? Actually, the Investment Company lost the money, I was only the portfolio manager and making bad decisions is not a crime.

It is well know, in the stock market a Company can lose money or make it, not the stock advisor or broker. Everyone investing accepts the fact that three things can happen. The

Investor makes money, losses money, or, his Investment is flat. The government claimed I told investor's investing in the stock market was "As Safe" as the Government. An absolute stupid thing for anyone to believe, or, say. The SIPC is "as safe" as the FDIC not the stock market.

I had a good track record in the Stock Market prior to 1980, and a bad one after that. I never intentionally invested in stock that would go down. I would not know how to do that.

Bryant told the jury, "Mr. Parris has been very candid with you, he has admitted losing the investors money."

The lawyer never called the employee of Merrill Lynch who hand carried the $32,000.00 check back to his employer on April 29, 1986. Nor, did Bryant call the jury's attention to the date of 4-29 on the deposit on the back of the $32,000 check. (It was deposited on April 29, 1986, the same day it was written and handed to me to deposit). Did Mrs. Milligan try to entrap me by asking me to mail this check for her? Pretty silly, right, but not more silly than all this garbage about inventing a way to lose money in the Stock Market.

Bryant failed to mention, or, present a copy of the One Million Dollar Fidelity Insurance Polity, the basis of Count II -"Mr. Parris falsely told Mrs. Ware, Over the phone, he had Insurance (wire fraud)."

Any person past the third grade would have presented the policy and call the insurance salesman. And, since it was "fidelity insurance" it might actually be used to show the Jury that no money was "diverted to Mr. Parris' personal use"—

The third and final count "*On May 20, 1986, Parris mailed Mrs. Ware a check in the amount of $800.00.*" I was gone from the Investment Company on May 16, 1986. *However, part of my job with the company required me to deposit investments in the company and send out checks to anyone who requested a withdrawal.* My contract with the Investment Company called for me to receive money and make deposits, and return funds to those who requested a withdrawal.

The three count indictment was for mailing a company deposit to the company's checking account, sending a company check to a investor/owner, who had requested the withdrawal, and answering a phone call from the investor who hadn't received the requested check on June 17, 1986. Mrs. Ware and the other owners of the Investment Company had already filed civil action on June 3, 1986. She was really calling to find out if they won the civil suit would I been able to pay them the $300,000 dollars they were claiming I had diverted to my personal use.

I said, "Mrs. Ware, I have a one million dollar fidelity insurance policy. I lost money in this Investment company, just like you; However, if you prove to a jury that I was dishonest in any way, I believe the insurance will be forced to pay you and all the others who lost money in the Stock Market."

Later, the Federal Government would prove to the Tenth Circuit Court of Appeals that I was "lulling" Mrs. Ware on June 17, 1986 (I know lulling is bad, but is it wire fraud, Or, a pattern of using the phone for the purpose of furthering a scheme? Maybe Mrs. Ware called me to lull Me.). I was gone from the Investment Company so; I couldn't have been furthering my scheme to intentionally lose her money in the stock market.

"Parris falsely told Mrs. Ware, over the phone, when she called him on June 17, 1986, that he had Insurance in order to *lull her* into not filing civil court action against him." *Mrs. Ware, and the others, had already filed civil court action on June 3, 1986.*

Bryant presents the 1984 Contract between the Investment Company and me. He then presented the

Company's By Law's that had been prepared for the owners by Attorney John Cripps.

The Insurance Policy and Seventy other documents were left out. (You have to wonder just how close the Circuit Court of Appeals look at the trial record). The fight to keep innocent people out of prison once allowed for cases such as this one to be out on bond until the appeal's process was over. It actually takes two years for some cases to obtain a ruling from the Court of Appeals. So, how much time just goes by with the file even being looked at and how much time do the Appeals Judges spend actually looking at the record? Innocent people should be allowed to go free until the Appeal's process is complete (i.e. in non-violent cases).

The Contract and By Law's were the Federal Government's exhibits 19 and 21. These two documents were the only exhibits presented by Mr. Bryant. He needed to actually present something, and what better way to make the Jury think I was more than the portfolio manager than my using the Owners two documents and make believe they were in my possession. That is killing two birds with one stone.

My answers to questions were more of attempt to tell the jury about all the things other people should have been asked. Arguing your case and testifying only confuses a jury and makes anything you say seem unimportant, and confusing. Knowing this fact did me no good. I was unable to control myself. I set through two days of seeing witnesses crying because they trusted me to make money for them.

One government witness (Bill Ed Brooks) admitted he knew my money was lost right along with his and the rest. I wonder if Charles Ponzi lost money in his scheme?

I managed to tell the Jury about the box of records my lawyer had *not* used, and some of the witnesses he never called. I told the jury, the government used my personal business checking account in Sallisaw, Oklahoma, as the Investment Company's instead of the real one in Fayetteville, Arkansas, for the purpose of using investor funds. Then, the same government used the real checking account in Fayetteville for the purpose of mailing a deposit.

The Government was forced to use my personal business checking account in order to show ten or fifteen personal checks as examples of my using the Investment Company funds to pay my personal bills. I had a feeling some of the jurors were ready to give me the benefit of the doubt!

Then, the government called my ex-daughter-in-law, Kathy Cottrell, as their only rebuttal witness. She said she saw me burn a bunch of records in my backyard and sign over a stack of, at least, twenty assets to my wife, Carol.

She was asked to lie and make me look like a liar. I told Craig Bryant to ask her how big my backyard was? It is ten feet from the backdoor to the back fence. I wanted Bryant to point out there are two burn barrel located behind the barn. The most likely place I would have used to burn papers, or anything else.

"The box of records she is saying I burned is right here. You never even bothered looking in it and now you see how the Fed's are using your ignorance." Bryant asked her the same thing the U.S. Attorney asked. (As he had done with all the other witnesses).

I said, "You said we were going to put on our case after the government finished, where is it?"

"You had better be quite and settle down, you are looking bad to the Judge and Jury with all your squirming around and loud talk." Bryant said

"You have already got me convicted, my only hope is that Judge Seay will see you did nothing in the way of a defense. It's got to help that I told him before the trial, that this is what you were going to do."

"The rebuttal witness is unimportant." Bryant said.

I said, "You think I'm stupid? That lying little bitch just made me look like a liar, and I am the only defense you presented. It don't matter what you do—the Judge is going to throw out this mess and let me have a fair trial."

"No way. And, you want get a reversal on appeal either." Bryant said.

"Get a lawyer and file an appeal, because this trial is over— Asshole." Bryant added.

I said, "god damn you sorry prick, you've made it easy for the Court to see what's going on here, you crooked little pimp faced sack of shit. The Judge can't be crooked like you and Raley

"You really are an idiot, don't you know the Judge is in on this conviction, smart guy?" Bryant said.

"No way a Federal Judge is going to stoop to ruining somebody's life, just to help a U.S. Senator pay me back. People tell me 'Seay is the best Federal Judge in Oklahoma.' You're crazy as hell."

During Agent Vest's testimony the Judge asked him to find one thing in the 70,000 papers, just so the Court would know Mr. Vest could find each document in the mass of papers. The Court asked Mr. Bryant to suggest what that one item should be. While he was looking, and not finding it. I walked over and asked him if the bank records for Parris Chevrolet was in those thousands of papers?

He said they were.

I asked him if the $250,000 Bank Notes from Commercial National Bank was in that bank account?

He said no they were not. "So, you found where I paid for Parris Chevrolet in that bank account, but failed to find the loan deposits?

What do you mean? Vest asked.

I mean the loan deposits, or the checks that repaid Commercial National for the loans.

What are you talking about? Vest asked.

The $250,000 in the Parris Chevrolet Checking Account Statement from the Bank in Muskogee and the transfer's to my checking account in Sallisaw and the canceled checks paying the contractors?"

"Yes that's right." Vest said.

"What is right?" I asked

"I mean I took all that into account." Vest said.

"Shit, that don't make no sense at all. What bout the $100,000 Airplane, you found canceled checks adding up to that much?"

"That is correct." Vest said.

"That is real interesting, just how many checks were written?"

"Six I believe there were six. Yes, I am sure there was six checks for eighteen thousand 500 each". Vest said.

Vest is built along the lines of a tall Tom Cruise. This must be the "look" the Justice Department wants, because the Fraud Division Lawyer from Washington has the same size, build, complexion, and hair cut. Vest majored in Accounting at a Phoenix, AZ. University. Says he got a degree. Six times 18,500 equal 100,000.

uh huh

"The $100,000 dollar dog, and $200,000 on the chevy dealership, were all items purchased in the last five month of 1984. And, I got the money to purchase them from my "*Victims*" in the Investment Company, is that a fair statement?"

Vest said, "something like that."

"What was the value of the Investment Company on August 1, 1984?"

"Easy, that would be $596,000." Vest answered.

"Let's see if I have this right? There was $596,000 in the account on August 1, 1984. I paid out $200,000, $100,000, and another $100,000. Only $32,000 was invested and Bill Ford took out $331,000. Deduct from this the $194,000 you said I lost in 1985-87. Do you thank that adds up?

Vest said, "Well, there were a couple of other deposits. Not much more, "Maybe two $10,000 and three $2,000."

"Okay, add another $26,000 to the investments and you think I would have been able to embezzle $100,000 for a Plane, $100,000 for the Dog, and $200,000 for the Chevy Deal. And, give Jackson back $52,500, Mrs. Ware $4,000, Mrs. Milligan $26,811. And, Lose $194,000 in the stock market. And still be able to hand $331.000 to Mr. Ford. Please, just tell me you are saying I could do all of this?"

Special Agent VEST walked off.

My personal business checking account in Sallisaw recorded $298,000 in deposits, other than loans, in 1984, 85, and 86. Sallisaw Greyhound Farm (Carol's business) recorded in excess of $435,000 for the same period. One deposit was in the amount of $50,000. Parris Chevrolet had deposits, before it opened for business, of $200,000 in October of 1984. After completion of the facility GMAC purchased the note from Commercial National Bank in Muskogee. I am sure any Accountant would have been able to find the bank loan deposits, repayments, and account for the breeding fees Carol collected.

To call this an honest mistake would be like the Emperor of Japan claiming his planes just got a little off course when they bombed pearl harbor.

These boys have set out to put me in prison. I Overheard Mr. Vest tell Mr. Bryant,

"I can't find that report, give me another one to look for.

"Forget about it, the Court want ask for it again."

"How about asking him to find two checks for $18,500 dollars. I'll plead guilty if he can do that.

Bryant was right, the Court did ask him to find another piece of paper amount the 70,000.

13

On June 5, 1991, at around 7 p.m. the jury delivered the expected verdict.—

Guilty on all three counts.

Mr. Bryant seemed pleased with the results of his performance.

Sentencing was set for August 1, 1991.

As I walked through the door of my home in Sallisaw, the phone was ringing.

"Hello…yes they convicted me on all three counts."

"Yes, I could get some jail time."

"Yes, I know my lawyer did a horrible job."

"Yes, I know you only told the truth as you saw it."

"Well I am sorry about the whole thing too."

"Okay, thanks for calling."

Two more owners called before 10 p.m. each saying virtually the same thing. "Your lawyer never asked me anything. He was really bad. Why did that FBI Agent lie?" We all felt bad about the experience of the last ten years (1981-91).

At 10 PM I called Anthony Puglisi in Tampa, Florida.

"Did I get you up?"

"No Bob, happy to hear from you. How did the trial go? Tony asked.

"You know there was only one way for it too go."

"You had a bad lawyer, I could have done more for you than he did." Tony said.

"Wish I could have visited with you for a little while."

"Me too, Bob, you was honest with me. We just had a kind of handshake deal that's all. The Track would have made me pay you 35% of the Dogs winnings, if you would have demanded it. I know you never intended to hurt those people. We got a bumper sticker going around down here that says 'Shit happens.' When I see it I think of you, sorry." Tony said.

"That's OK, Tony, that about sums it up for me too."

After I hung up, Mr. Craig called and the first thing he said was, "your lawyer was just awful, I never seen anything like it. He tried his best to get me to say you bought the dog."

"I know, it was insane." I said.

"You know, I remember your wife gave me a cashier check for the Fifty Thousand dollars. It was written at a Muskogee Bank, I think. It's just been so long ago. I didn't know you guys at the time, and I wanted a cashier check. Didn't want to drive all the way back to Kansas with all that much cash, and didn't want to worry about a bad check."

I said, "It was your and Carol's deal. I was around, ready to help, if I was needed for anything."

"She made good money breeding Toby, and I am glad for her. The dog will be in the hall of fame. Toby and his brothers and sisters made me a lot of money at the racetrack, and they have all produced wonderful babies. I am proud for the dog, he was the greatest greyhound I ever saw, and I been in the business more than fifty years." Mr. Craig said.

14

On June 10, 1991 (five day after the illegal trial) at 3:12 PM, I filed a motion for Trial DeNovo (new trial) and listed seventy-six errors made by the Court Appointed U.S. Public Defender, along with the ninety-two documents and the eight witnesses not present in my defense. My right to an impartial jury was violated. I never mentioned all the misconduct (conspiracy) of the Government because I still couldn't believe all these mistakes were overt acts.

It took me longer to type the case number on the motion than it took the honorable Frank Howell Seay to review the motion and deny it.

It was filed within the ten-day period for filing for a new trial and it deserved a hearing, at the very least. Especially considering Judge Seay was told before the trial: (1) my lawyer has not even looked at the box of evidence I want presented in my defense. And (2) my lawyer has not filed a subpoena for any of the eight witnesses I want called to testify on by behalf.

I called Mr. Green and Mr. Stipe about doing the appeal and was advised I would need to bring $25,000 into Mr. Stipe's office. Mr. Green was about to become part of Mr. Raley's staff.

Dan Draper said he would do it for $5,000, and I sent it to him.

Draper could have had the sentencing postponed until he was up to speed on the case, but failed to present anything, not even make his entry of appearance.

On August 1, 1991, Bryant stood up with me as if he was my Attorney, or something.

I said, "This man didn't even try to defend me, your honor, why is he standing here beside me like I have a Lawyer."

"Your lawyer did a fine job. All you have done since this trail started is bad mouth your trial counsel, and it's going to cost you some extra time now." The Honorable Judge said.

I said, "fine job? Sorry, your honor, I think he helped the government and did nothing for me. Do you realize I was convicted of *intentionally losing money in the stock market*? Some of it mine and my families?"

The Court: "five years for count I. five years for count II, and, five more for count III, all to run consecutively for a fifteen year period. Mr. U.S. Marshall take this man into custody, next case.

"I looked at Mr. Bryant and said, "You said I could get as much as three years. Mr. Raley said in the newspaper that I could get as much as five. What is this? A first time offender of a $32,800 scheme gets an all time record high sentence of fifteen years.

"Hell, this gives you one more thing to bitch about, don't it." Bryant said.

The Court: "Marshall's I said take charge of this prisoner Now."

Over fifty-five years of living, I have witnesses many horrible events, both in person and on TV, but the look in my wife and daughter's eye's when my hands were handcuffed behind my back, tops the list. The best actor in Hollywood could not duplicate the terror in their eyes. You walk into a fire you expect to get burned, when a committee of honorable men conspire to punish you for their own pleasure and revenge its harder to accept.

FBI Agent, Tom Vest, fabricated bank and brokerage firm records and testified too their truthfulness and accuracy. Vest heard Mr. Ford testify there was no Audit of the company records.

It took Vest two years to admit he lied to the jury. It only took U.S. Attorney, John Raley, two month to admit he conspired to fabricate evidence, knowingly presented false documents and perjured testimony. He admitted knowing Vest and the ex-daughter-in-law were committing perjury at the time.

U.S. Public Defender, Craig Bryant, knowingly allowed false evidence to be presented. He had in his possession documents to impeach them, and his failure to use this exculpatory evidence, makes him a criminal in my way of thinking.

Our system of justice requires honesty at the highest level. Fail this requirement, and we get what happened at Waco and the retaliation at Oklahoma City. Fail this foundation for justice and you have children killing each other in our public school. Justice begins in the Courts and ends up in the streets and school yard's of America.

The Federal Government has taken Over State court's jurisdiction and proved they are just as sorry and corrupt, older people have too much prejudice to see the truth, but young minds easily see this slime and react.

Present a lifetime job to a human being with no peer pressure and you get little kingdoms like the Judge Seay has in Muskogee.

David Lyle Boren, former Oklahoma House Member, Governor, U.S. Senator, and. now, the President of the University of Oklahoma, used the power of his office for personal vengeance by having his appointee's send an innocent man to prison.

Using the power the people gave him in this kind of way should cause him to spend eternity in a very warm place but I am not his judge. If fact, I forgive him and Judge Seay for their arrogance.

A week in Prison is more than "doughboy" would last. The University of Oklahoma should get a president the sports program and student body can be proud of.

The dishonest government officials are up to five: Boren, Vest, Bryant, Raley, and the Special Attorney with the Fraud Division of the Federal Bureau of Investigation Branch of the United States Department of Justice in Washington, DC.

WOW…I was impressed the first time he rattled all that off to me.—Gomer Pyle comes to mind. You know, when he says gaaooolllieeee. All of that other stuff, and he's from Washington, DC.

I wanted so bad to tell him "Well I am shore glad to meet you, I am Special Citizen of the Cherokee Nation and founder of many things great and small from Short, Oklahoma. Thank you very little."

When I was in the Navy at Norfolk, Va., a sailor would do something bad and all of us would suffer.

15

"Dogs and Sailor's keep of the grass" were on yard signs all around Norfolk. The actions of a few bad apples will pollute the system if we ignore them, or allow them to continue their work of rotting America from the inside.

The Two hundred 25 pound Indian girl was being dragged and pushed into the Muskogee County Jail by three members of the Muskogee County Sheriff's office. She had a thin little line of blood running out of her oversized nose. It trickled down her dark brown face in a steady stream. Eventually the red blood merged with her light blue dress and changed to a faded maroon color.

She was drunk and being very unruly, or, as the police would say, disorderly with the police officer's. The pants had one leg missing and the crotch had been ripped out. Two guards from the Jail joined in the attempt to hog tie the girl, but they could never quite get her under control. Finally, the five men manage to wrestle her into a dressing room in front of the booking window.

The police gave up on tying her down and just strip her cloths off a hand full at a time. She was pushed back out of the small room and through the iron door to the drunk-tank, which had a cluster of cells. The Indian girl had no cloths on she was naked as a Jay bird (As we used to say as we swam in Lees Creek in the raw).

On Monday mornings the tank is generally empty. There are six cells around a turn out area, each cell holds upwards of ten drunks (more when pressed). The turn out area in the middle connects all the cells in a square kind of deal. The central area could hold another fifty or sixty people, if necessary.

The iron bared six by eight door to the sixth cell had been removed and a shower stall and drain were added. This rebuilt cell is in the corner nearest the booking room.

The Indian girl swatted and kicked at the two guards and three police deputies as they moved her to the inside booking room window. She dipped and ducked around as the police pinched her butt and rubbed her tits and grabbed her inside the crotch area. The men clearly were having fun. Laughing like someone had told a big joke or something.

The man in the booking room gave her a bottle of liquid soap with chemicals to keep lice from getting off her and into the prison population. It had the smell of rotten eggs.

"Shower, soap down with this, then shower again. Be sure you get this soap all over everything except in your eyes." The supply officer said.

The blond deputy, with bad teeth, took the bottle as they shoved the big girl into the concrete shower room. Three guys had brown hair and could have weighed as much as the girl. the other man was almost bold and might have tipped the scales at a hundred and fifty pounds. He was likely above fifty and the other four couldn't be past thirty. The girl calmed down as the men put her under the shower and stopped trying to move her around. She stood there with both hands raised above her and against the concrete wall.

She appeared to be going to sleep as these men applied the liquid over her big body. Then, the men begin doing more than smearing the soap, and chemicals, on her—she started punching and bellowing. For a big girl she could jump pretty high and move quicker than one might expect.

A wild swing caught one of the dark hared men in the middle of his face and likely broke his nose.

This is when the nightsticks came into play. In the beginning of the shower stall adventure the five men sort of took turns rubbing the girl. Being careful to not get their cloths and shoes wet. Sort of a stand off and control a couple of feet from the water. Now, Two men pounded her fat body with their nightsticks and the other three were doing there best to get their hands/fingers inside vagina. Three guys, six hands, thirty fingers all trying to get in the same area of the girls body. They are all getting soaked.

She fell to the concrete floor on her back, and begins kicking and moving herself around in a circle by using her elbows. The bass in her voice, started sounding more high pitched like a cat with its tail caught and couldn't get loose.

Finally, the Jailer in charge came out of the booking room.

"You guys better lighten up, the Feds brought in a new prisoner and I got him waiting over in cell one. He can see most of what you guys are doing in here."

While the men were talking and looking in my direction, the girl managed to get to her feet. She bowed her back and charged like a bull. The force of her big fat body knocked the short bald headed guard up against the wall. He sounded like air brakes going off on a big truck.

The Indian Girl was moving even better now that she was sobering up a little. She started off to the left and suddenly whirled around, pinning the blond guard up in a corner. She held him by his belt buckle, picking him up some. She moved her head back a little and brought it down against the blond guard's head. He dropped to the concrete floor when she turned loose of the belt.

She ran back across the shower room and busted another deputy on the side of the head. He went crashing backward over another Law Enforcement Officer and fell onto the floor.

A club landed square on the back of her head. It sounded like a baseball bat hitting a watermelon. She went down hard. I knew she was dead. But, when they rolled her onto her back I could hear the screech in her heavy breathing.

The boys spread her out, and begin using the sticks on her two at a time, one in the front and one in the rear. Then, two in front and one in the rear. (I saw more violence committed by the police my first hour in prison than I had witnessed in my entire life).

The water running on top of this group of law enforcement officers, prison guards, and one female prisoner turned red as it entered the drain, some of it was from the law boys, but most of it belonged to the seventeen-year-old Indian Girl.

I started screaming for them to stop. "For God's sake, what kind of people are you?

16

The Federal section of the Muskogee County Jail was on the north side of the third floor, In portions of two large and two small units. Twenty inmates could be put in the large units and ten in the small ones. Each unit had an open area with a TV and concrete tables. The bed is metal and the mattress is the thickness of a dime and no pillow. A few minutes on each side and the metal bed has your entire body aching. You lay on it as long as you can then get up and watch "*soul train*" or "*Up all Night*" on the USA network.

The glass on the Cell Door magnifies and reflects the entire cell so the guards can see you at all times. You potty and shower in front of everyone.

The other inmates are friendlier than stories you hear or read about. The Dormitory door is opened and you line up for your food tray. At mail call you can hand in your commissary list (if you have money in your commissary account). Candy and Chips make up 90% of the things offered.

Four people are eligible to visit each prisoner for ten minutes twice a week. For visits you are brought to a 4'x4' concrete box with a thick glass window to look at your visitor through and a phone to communicate with them on. There are four telephones in each dormitory. You have to call outside collect. The extra charge for a prison call is $12.00, plus 38 cents a minute, just another way families of prisoners are punished. A call averages costing the family or friend $32.00 each.

The first inmate I talked too was Bruce (his last name, I can't remember his first name). Mr. Bruce was a local boy from a rich family. He had a mental problem. He signed a gun purchase form. One of the items asked on the form was if you were ever a patient in a mental hospital. Mr. Bruce lied on the form and he is in prison with me. This is a good example of people with money being in a Federal Prison. His family could come down and get him out anytime. None of the other poor prisoners have that option. Mr. Bruce was a large man in his early twenties. The inmates living in the Muskogee area say he was the smartest guy in school.

He was friendly, and I liked him right off. When he had mental problems they medicated him with Thorizene and he walked around stiff legged, mumbling to himself for a couple of hours. When they gave him too much he would sleep all the time.

I found out Judge Seay sent him to the mental ward at Springfield, Missouri. What he needed was to go home. He was never violent and purchased that gun to going hunting with his friends.

His parents might think he would be better cared for in a controlled environment but these people could care less about helping him. They just give him enough medication to make sure he is no problem. When he finally gets to go home, his brain will be burned up completely.

Dale Snider was another inmate I met the first day. He liked a month serving a ten-year sentence for armed robbery. He and his fifteen-year-old sister were working there way across the Country from Indiana to California.

Dale said he and his sister worked four hours for a farmer. The man fed them and they worked five more hours. They were to get $10.00 each, at the end of the day.

"Supper and Lunch is all I'm gonna pay." The Farmer said.

Dale got his gun out of the bag and forced the farmer to hand over $26.00.

Within an hour Dale and his sister were in jail. He fed the pigs at El Reno Federal Prison for ten years and was ready to be released when the guard slipped a half-pint of whiskey to celebrate his freedom. The next thing Dale says he remembers is asking a gas station attendant in Rudy, Arkansas which way it was to El Reno, Oklahoma. Dale Snider's medicine had a reaction with the whiskey and Dale spent two days in the twilight zone. He forced a lady in El Reno to drive him back to Indiana. In Rudy, Arkansas Dale needed to go to the bathroom. While he was gone the lady called the police. The woman was unharmed.

Dale is waiting his day in Court. Later, I found out he saved his medication until his court date and took them all at once. He just wanted to prove to Judge Seay what this could do to him and save him the kidnapping part of the charge.

Who knows what the whole story is? What's clear form what I saw of this case, the Public Defender failed to fill this poor man in on the best was to solve his legal problems. He said he was 29 years old, but he acted more like 9.

To me no sane person spends ten years in prison and escapes with a month to go. They should have let him communicate with his sister. He spent most of his time worrying about her.

Some state prisoners were mixed in with us higher paying federal customers. The State of Oklahoma paid $35.00 dollars a day, and the Fed's paid $65.00.

We had a State guy who could have been a millionaire businessman. He was brilliant. The only thing that excited him was getting away with something illegal. He got caught with seventy-three different company checks from the Tulsa Area. He had a bundle of blank Oklahoma Drivers License and an official photo machine.

He would write a payroll check to Joe Blow, make a picture ID of himself as Joe Blow, and cash it anywhere. This is what they caught him doing. I suspect he was doing a lot more illegal things. During the trial the District Attorney told the jury that this guy was the man with a thousand faces and names.

Let's see we had two boys from Canada. They were in for selling automatic weapons in the U.S. The Fed's decked these two young men (skinny) gunrunners out in very loud clothing and let them return to Canada.

The Phone call one of them made to their leader in Canada said, "I will come to Buffalo, NY and pick you boys up."

The Fed's made them stand out in a crowd so they could easily spot them in Buffalo, NY. They wanted the boss gunrunner.

The boys came around to where we could see them from our third floor window and waved to us from the street. We were laughing at the red pants and blue shirts these boys were wearing, and those prep school beanie caps, Wow. The guard came in a laughed with us.

Then he told us what the deal was. The Fed's wanted the guy from Canada to cross the border. The scheme included an informant visiting the boys with a "secure" cell phone. I guess they fell for it.

Thirty guys in my pod and each one with a story. I called my new Attorney, Dan Draper. I had been in prison twenty minutes and it seemed like 20 days.

"When are you coming down?" I ask.

"The motion for release pending the appeal is being set, and I will be down tomorrow."

I said, "Great, I'm dying here. Being away from home is like being held down with a five hundred-pound boulder, your body just wants to explode and all directions at once."

"I'll be down tomorrow and hopefully we will be getting you out in two weeks."

I said, "I'm telling you, time is counted in seconds, not hours or weeks. Do what you can as fast as possible, please."

A hearing was finally held on October 12, 1991. Two months and twelve days I've suffered every second of every long day and night. Draper couldn't do anything with the Appeal to the Tenth Circuit because he needed the evidence he was going to present at the Hearing to make a record for our Appeal.

"There is nothing much in the Court record of your trial to show the Appeal's Court" Draper, said.

At the hearing, Draper presented two witnesses who testified they had known me for a long time and I was not likely to flee. Nine documents were shown the Honorable Judge Seay impeaching the entire government case.

The government admitted to the Honorable Judge they knowingly presented false testimony and fabricated evidence. The Investment Company lost the money in the stock market Mr. Parris never diverted any money to his personal use.

Mr. Draper showed the Court it would have been foolish for Mr. Parris to run home and "sign a stack of assets to his wife, Carol", in advance of the Civil Court Action filed June 3, 1986, because Carol J. Parris was a party to the Court Action. (The plaintiff's could collect from the Wife the same as the Husband) the bank account was wrong, so there was no commingling of funds. The percentages quoted to the investor/owners by Mr. Parris were, in fact, correct. All the funds were accounted for and none was diverted to Mr. Parris' personal use. $331,000 was in the Investment Company's Account at Merrill Lynch & Co., including the last deposit of $32,000. Pretty much eliminating the government's theory that Mr. Parris needed this "victim" or "Cash Cow" to give him her life savings so he could go out and throw it away in the Stock Market for her. The other "Senior Citizen" involved in the Investment Company was my grandmother. When she was 90 years old, she gave all the kids $25,000. All she wanted was the interest off this amount until she died. I had put my sister's, Claudine, and my money in the Investment Company. I later purchased some propane tanks and let my sister's husband, Paul Laney, manage them, and he took over the $20,000 dollar mortgage.

The newspaper made quite a thing of me beating my own grandmother out of her life savings. It was my $25,000 that was lost, and she left her two living sons and three living daughters in excess of $200,000 each.

The same Honorable Judge from my illegal trial is hearing this motion. He now has all the information necessary to release me pending the Appeal. He actually has enough information to reverse his denial of my motion for a new trial, filed five days after the corrupt trial.

Three months in the worst kind of prison should be enough to satisfy my opposition. I set in the County Prison until November 23, 1991, before Judge Seay denied my motion.

The Judge now knows almost everything about the Government's case were false and fabricated.

Was Mr. Bryant right about this Judge? On December 12, 1991, I was shipped from the Holdover Unit at El Reno, to the Federal **Correction** Institution (FCI) in LaTuna.

17

The world is a small place and full of unusual happenings. One year ago to the day from the time I arrived in LaTuna, I was on I-10 going from Phoenix to El Paso. Heading home from delivering a load of Carol's dogs to the Greyhound track in Phoenix. I decided to visit Tombstone, El Paso, and other areas of interest along the southern border with Mexico. What's unbelievable is that as I passed the New Mexico/Texas Border I looked up the hill and saw this lovely Old Spanish Style Church campus. I couldn't see the razor wire from the Intestate.

One year later, I am getting a closer look at this miserable place and there is nothing lovely about it.

Christmas in FCI LaTuna was a Mexican disaster. Two weeks behind the razor wire, and I was a candidate for the Nut Farm. Ever wonder what it would like? Try living in a pool hall

24 hours a day. Get a hard cot, two-inch thick pillow. Put the cot in a corner of the pool hall and listen to pool balls clash and people yelling half the night.

LaTuna is about twenty miles from El Paso, at a place called Anthony, NM/TX. Cactus, that's what LaTuna means in Spanish. Just add sand and you have a complete description of this place. It's four miles to the Mexican Border. Each cell holds four people and opens into a large area with four pool tables and six card tables. On weekdays the cue ball whacked the other balls until 10 p.m., on weekends they are whacked all night long.

Black people love to slam down a domino. I fail to know the reason they do this, but it's a fact. Try it some time. Get a domino and bring it up as far as your arm will go and wham it down on the table as forceful as possible. At the same time you must scream as loud as possible, motherfucker, take that you motherfucking, motherfucker.

White prisoners try to impersonate a Black guy doing these things, but fail miserably.

Mexicans don't even make the effort.

LaTuna is 70% Mexican, 20% black and 10% white. Before I arrived in LaTuna, a person who is now one of my cellmates made a successful escape. He cut through the wire and had about an hour's head start. The guards were still about a mile behind, as he crossed the Rio Grande into Mexico. Instead of keeping on running, he stopped and started giving them the finger, and laughing.

When he realized they were coming across the river, and begin running again, it was too late, they caught him a mile inside Mexico.

"You can't come into Mexico. You got no Jurisdiction." He yelled over and over.

He was still yelling, telling me about it two years later

"They can't fucking do that, can they?"

I said, "they can do anything they want to do, right or wrong, you shouldn't have stopped?"

"Thanks, I will remember that next time."

The old HACK who ran the broom factory for Unicor came by the Law Library and talked me into working in the Unicor office.

I had a heart attack when I was in Muskogee. This left me with a work restriction pass. I told him I would do his accounting if I could use the computer to type legal brief's after hours. It was a good paying job (25 cents per hour) and the legal work made me a dollar a page.

The Mexicans and Blacks were at each other all the time. One night I woke up sometime after midnight. The three Mexican's who shared a cell with me were up and trying to be very quite. They usually make as much racket as possible even in the middle of the night. After they were gone, I got up and followed them upstairs.

Whack, Whack, Whack, not too loud, more like a car going over a wooden bridge very slow. Five more men were with my three cellmates when they came out of the room carrying a limp black inmate. They were headed toward the shower with him. I went over and looked into the room and found two other black inmates knocked out on their bunks and taped down. One of the men in the four-man cell had moved out a few days ago and no replacement had arrived.

I went back to my room thinking that boy was gonna get screwed. The 4 a.m. rounds turned up two dead prisoners in the upstairs shower. They had been stabbed more than ten time each. When they gave their names we all knew these were the two guys who had just arrived from the prison at Big Springs. Word around LaTuna was these two black prisoners hurt a Mexican prisoner at Big Springs bad enough that he was still in a coma.

Twenty-seven black prisoners were taken to Receiving and Disbursing (R & D) and shipped out.

They always had a problem with inmates taking fruit and sugar out of the cafeteria. To combat this problem, two hacks would pat you down as you filed out of food service. Sometimes a female hack would be doing this, and all the prisoners would get in her line.

I was working in the Unicor Office, typing on my appeal. Not knowing all the units were locked down and no movement were being allowed. After I completed the work and started back to my Unit, I noticed that I was the only person moving around. Then, I saw all the dead pigeon's in the courtyard. The hacks fed them poisoned grain, and were scooping them into trash sacks. I was gonna caught hell for being out of bounds, until I promised never to tell what I had witnessed and went back to my unit.

The inmates had been carrying bread out of food service and feeding the pigeon's in the courtyard. To stop this, the birds were all killed.

The next morning, I overheard some prisoners asking what happened to the birds. I said, "They went north for the winter."

Before the day was out, everyone knew what happened, but not from me. Seeing a thousand birds in a sixty by seventy foot Spanish style courtyard continues to bother my sleep, even today.

Another silly thing the Fed's did was to camouflage the tennis courts. People were flying over the prison and seeing the tennis courts and making a fuss about these prisoners are living the life of luxury. The warden's all over America were ordered to put up basketball goals at the end of the tennis courts and paint the concrete like a basketball key. From the air, the tennis court looked like a small basketball court.

Rook and Troy were from the Little Rock area. Rook owned two or three furniture stores in Central Arkansas. And Troy had a business called "*Toys by Troy.*" Rook had a drug problem that was eating up all his profit. He went back to his mother, who ran a bank, in Conway, Arkansas, for an additional loan. She refused to loan him anymore money until he straightened up his life.

Rook and Troy picked up some guns and attempted to rob Rook's mothers' bank. Things when wrong and Rook killed the bank's robot in frustration.

These two were the characters at LaTuna. And, I know I'm in trouble for not telling the "Robot Story" right. Rook used the gun and got five more years than Troy.

I took Troy's place in Accounts payable at the Unicor Broom Factory. He went home three months after I arrived.

Rook had five more years to go, so; he's out there some-place...lookout.

The activity club elected Rook president. He stole all the club's T-shirts and sold them to the other inmates at half price.

I had met two guys in the Muskogee County Jail that were now in LaTuna.

Jim Spear was from Seminole, Oklahoma, and was in for manufacturing a machine gun.

Jim claims his wife turned him in. According to him, he called the Deputy Sheriff, and told him about the modified gun he had made just playing around.

"It will be all right as long as you don't attempt to sell it." He was told.

After the divorce, the same Deputy arrested him and turned him over to the Feds. Jim says his wife and the Deputy had a thing going.

The other inmate I had met earlier in Muskogee was Randy "whitie" Whitely from Idabel, Oklahoma. Randy had been a hard drug user. He moved from Kansas City back home to Idabel to help him get off drugs. He claims a guy ran off owing him rent and took his TV. Randy says the guy forgot about a He gun he had hidden in the loft. Trying to sell that gun to get some of his money back, is when the law got Randy.

About four month after I arrived in LaTuna, Randy was caught messing with the Education Teacher, a small, skinny, little woman about twenty years older than Randy. He spent two weeks in the hole and was shipped out. The Teacher was fired.

Jim Spear introduced me to his cellmate, Clyde Gray. Clyde had to be the largest white man in a Federal prison. Clyde was 6'10" and weighed more than 320 pounds. He was thick, solid, and not a bit of fat on him. He was convicted of stealing cars and chopping them up. His operation extended from Little Rock to Wichita.

He says, in the few months before being caught his business managed to steal two hundred cars a week and chop them up in either Wichita or Little Rock. They shipped parts all over the United States and Canada.

LaTuna was a medium security prison behind the wall and there were two camps outside that were minimum security. Clyde turned down re-assignment to the camp.

"Are you fucking crazy?" I asked one morning as we were walking the track.

"No, It's to easy to walk off and if I do that I will get another 3-5 years added onto my sentence. Besides—time goes faster inside the razor wire, than out in a camp." He replied, in his redneck slow southern draw of his.

We help each other pass a lot of prison time, walking the track and talking about things we did as young boys in Arkansas and Oklahoma. I hardly ever talked to him about my wife, kids, and grand kids, because I was about the only prisoner who still had any of that left. Clyde and most of the other two thousand inmates at LaTuna checked their families at the door when they entered the Federal Prison System. It was painful for them to talk about.

18

The appeal Dan Draper was going to file for me in November '91, remained on hold into March '92. I finally got permission to make a call to the 10th Circuit Court of Appeals in Denver, Colorado. They advised me the appeal had been stricken for lack of activity. Nothing had been filed for six months and application for an extension had not been requested.

I knew Dan had a drinking problem, and I shouldn't have trusted my life to someone with that problem.

Dan Draper found me another Attorney. Tom Stephenson filed to re-open my appeal, and promised Dan he would do a good job for the $5,000 Dan handed over to him.

The main information I wanted the 10th Circuit to see was the transcript of the Hearing Judge Seay allowed Mr. Draper to have on October 12, 1991. And the Court's Ruling denying my release pending the Appeal.

The Judge saw the Insurance Policy and the Fabricated Accounting Figures. And, U.S. Attorney, John Raley, admitted there was actually an Insurance Policy, his accounting figures were in error, no money was diverted, and the bank account location was incorrect. The false pretense was not false. And, he knew the Rebuttal Witness was committing perjury. Raley knew Bill Ford and Tom Vest were also committing perjury. He knew the check for $32,000 was actually not mailed.

Judge Seay found the three hours Craig Bryant spent reviewing the case with me was the important thing presented at this hearing. In his order denying release on bond while the appeal was going forward.

"There are any number of trial strategy reasons" why Craig Bryant chose to not present these documents. Judge Seay ruled.

The only trail strategy offered by the government, at the hearing, was the close proximity of the asset transfer to my wife, Carol, to the filing of the Civil Action might preclude the Defense Attorney from wanting to show the rebuttal witness was committing perjury. What a crock of shit!

The time spent was the only thing presented that anyone could argue about. All the other things were reversible error and Judge Seay knew it. After the Hearing, and before I received the Order. I told Dan Draper

"Even this dishonest Judge like Frank Howell Seay will have to release me after seeing all this corruptible evidence."

Dan said, "Just the Insurance Policy ends the government's entire theory. It's existence ends count II, and being Fidelity Insurance ends any idea that you used investor funds, or, intentionally created a scheme to defraud the owners of the Investment Company. The Judge will likely order a new trial and this thing will be over."

Of course, Judge Seay issued his senseless ruling a month later.

In the last week of November '91, I was in the Holdover Unit at El Reno, OK. Not to far from Dan's home in Stillwater. We all thought I would be out on bond during the appeal, or, are given two weeks to clear up my business before reporting to the prison at El Reno. SEAY felt it was urgent for me to be put away. Maybe people will stop losing money in the Stock Market, if I am locked up.

I clearly believe SEAY had an orgasm as he sentenced me. The way his face quivered and his eyes twitched from almost shut to wide open, and his breathing became labored and raspy. Hitler must have had much the same reaction as he put the Jews where his kind of law required them too be.

We must all strive to enjoy our work. Enjoying ruining other people's lives may be going a little too far.

Before the ruling, my wife, Carol, said she could tell a difference in Dan Draper, when she talked to him over the phone.

He accepted a collect call from me on December 1, 1991.

I said, "Carol said you still had some things to do before filing the Appeal."

"Yes, I am looking for a couple of documents to put with it." Draper said.

"I thought you had two months to get everything except the October hearing transcript ready."

"I've been fairly tied up with lobbying activities lately, but I will get it filed in two weeks." He said.

I said, "Can you believe the Judge's order?"

"That's just him, he believes you did these bad things and loopholes are not going to keep you from paying." Draper answered.

"Bill Ford went all over Sallisaw telling everyone he called Senator Boren and told him this was his last chance to the man who pulled the flag down."

"They are both from Seminole, and David got him appointed, but I know Frank to be the most honest person in the world?"

I said, "Rep. Barker told me you and Judge Seay were roommates, but I never knew for sure. Didn't help in my case, did it? Anyway, I am here for a week or two before going all the way down to near El Paso, can you come over?"

"I'll make ever effort, there are some things we need to look at together, I guess." He said

Four months later, I am still stuck in prison waiting for my lawyer to file the appeal.

Dan Draper would not accept my collect calls in 1992, so; I asked my Cousin, Fred, to kick his ass for failing to file the appeal.

"I paid him $5,000.00 where is he?" I asked Fred.

Dan told Fred he had to proceed with his lobbying in the Oklahoma Legislature. He believed he could get the Appeal filed before the end of the year, when he accepted the job and it just took more time than he was able to put into it.

I said, "Did you ask him why he kept telling Carol he was just a few days away from filing it?"

"He said he never told her that." Fred replied.

"We found out from the Appeals Court, he never even filed for an extension of time to file, how long was he going to let me set in this stinking hell hole of a prison before he was going to tell us this bit of news?"

He says Tom Stephenson will do a good job and he would give him the $5,000, but you will have to sign some papers releasing him and requesting the Appeals Court to recognize Tom as your new Attorney." Fred said.

"God be praised, yes! Anything to end this misery as fast as possible. Just tell Tom to send me the papers."

19

After setting in line waiting for the phone over an hour, I was interrupted as I reached for the receiver by a very tall black guy.

"I'm next." He said.

"What are you talking about? It's my turn."

Black Charley jerked the phone to his chest and turned to dial. I hit him with a force I never knew I had in me, and knocked the tall motherfucker to the floor. The hack grabbed me before the skinny kid could get up and kill me.

After we got out of the Hole, we became friends. Black Charley was a good basketball player. Any college in the Country would have loved to have him in their lineup, but here he is with me. He got fifteen years for selling coke to Federal Officer of the Law.

The Federal Prison System has a rule that requires an inmate involved in a fight, be transferred. We got past this rule, somehow. When they reviewed my records a mistake was found. I was a minimum-security prisoner in a medium security prison.

"We can put you in the Camp here, or ship you to the Federal Prison Camp (FPC) Texarkana." My case manager said.

"How about FPC El Reno? That's closer to home"

"No room" she said.

"Okay, put me in the camp here."

Two weeks later, Tom Stephenson pulled some strings with his buddy, U.S. Senator Boren, and got me shipped to FPC El Reno.

Yes, this is my new lawyer. The Appeal is only two weeks away from being filed—How many times have I heard that? I have seen three people killed by other inmates and two by the guards. The physical danger is not what makes me the most interested in getting the appeal filed and getting out. It's my wife, kids, and grandchildren. I need to see them.

And, of course, the mental damage is always present it is eating away at you from the inside. All the inmates worry about how much of a brain will be left when they finally get out.

After a year of this shit, time becomes more of an hour to hour thing, instead of a second by second claw the wall deal. After three years an hour is more of a day to day movement. You wonder how long before a month makes no difference, or a year?

In October '92, Tom Stephenson sends me a copy of the Appeal. It is a large filing of the Trial transcript, and makes the point that the scheme had reached fruition before the three counts of fraud were committed. "Parris' scheme (if there ever was one) was over before 1986. And, nothing Parris did in 1986, was in furtherance of a scheme." Did my new attorney win with this point?

The government's answer—it was "Lulling." Parris committed all those crimes from 1980 through 1985, and was "Lulling" the owners of the Investment Company into not filing Court Action against him.

"Parris took Mrs. Milligan's $32,000 dollar because he needed a "Cash Cow."

On May 20, 1986, Parris mailed Mrs. Ware a company check in the amount of $800.00 to "Lull" her into not filing court action.

Then, again on June 17, 1986, Parris told Mrs. Ware, over the phone, "I have insurance they will be contacting you within a week."

The Government says this activity was actually "lulling" her into not filing the court action she has already filed?

Now, it's hard to keep calling people names and not get the feeling that you are becoming a little paranoid. Tom Stephenson failed to use any of the evidence presented at the October '91 Hearing, which Mr. Draper waited six months to get before doing anything to further the appeal.

So far my evidence has been allowed to see the light of day. I called Tom and was surprised he accepted the collect call.

I said, "Tom, what happened to all the evidence from the bond hearing? You know nothing was presented in my favor, at the trial. The Appeals Court would have to release me, if they are shown the misconduct of everyone and violation of the "Brady" Evidence that was withheld. The illegal trial want have any record of this dishonesty."

"I thought I did a very good job of showing the Court there could be no Intent and therefore no crime." Tom said.

I said, yes you did a good job if I would have had a fair trial and my evidence would have been presented. Please file a supplemental and use the Fabricated evidence, Perjury, and Conspiracy evidence. The Federal Prosecutor, FBI Agent,

Federal Public Defender, and maybe even the Judge are all crooks."

"No can do, Bob, I have to work with the Federal Justice People on a daily basis. If I called your trial a sham, every Federal Employee in this Circuit would hang me. Think about trying to plea bargain with a Federal Prosecutor after calling one of them a coconspirator. My Legal career would be over, if I used any of the stuff from that hearing."

I said, "You left out David Lyle Boren. You do anything against him and you can kiss you ass goodbye too - right?"

"Right as rain my man, gotta go, bye." He hung up on me.

I spent the next week typing up a supplemental to the appeal. The Appeals Court sent it back. They cannot accept pleadings from non-lawyers unless they are pro se. I refilled the supplemental and advised the Court that Tom Stephenson no longer represented me.

Six months later, the Appeals Court issued its Order. Stealing all that money was found to be a crime. $889,008 was a lot of money to steal from our older citizens. Shame on you. Commingling funds were found to be a crime. Telling the investor's capital gains are 50% tax deductible is false. Telling the investor's dividends between corporations are 85% tax deductible is false. Telling the investor's the stock market is as safe as the government is unconscionable. Falsely telling the lady that you had Insurance is a brutal crime.

But, "Lulling" these people on June 17, 1986 into not filing a lawsuit on June 3, 1986, and mailing a check for the owner of the company is the most atrocious of all crimes in this Country.

It was the opinion of the Appeals Court that the Supplemental Filing was ambiguous and could not be understood. The three-judge panel (one each from Utah, Colorado and New Mexico) could not understand Perjury, or Fabricated Evidence, false documents, conspiracy, or judicial misconduct.

The Prosecutor's admission that no money had been stolen and they used the wrong bank account had no bearing on the stealing or commingling facts. All the evidence in the Box of Records not used by the Federal Public Defender was just beyond the comprehension of these judges from Utah, Colorado, and New Mexico. And, they do not know the IRS Code very well.

I said, "Maybe I should have used German or some other language for these guys."

"The three judges never even took the time to look at your appeal. The Prosecutor in Muskogee sent the Court Clerk, in Denver, a draft of what the Order should be. It saves a lot of time.

Hire Gene Stipe pay him $25,000. And they will suddenly understand your entire pleading, it will become clear as a bell and you will be out of here."

I said, "They let me out for a couple of hours and I will have the money, is that what this Country has come too? Commit a crime to save your ass from Prison for a crime you didn't committed?"

"You are going to do the time, and there is nothing else you can do about it. Once you are trapped in the Federal Justice System it's over."

"I know, but it makes me feel like I am not taking it setting down. I promised the Court Clerk in Denver I would be filing something the day I die, and I will." Bill Ford got all the money and is seeing a shrink about it.

20

It is well documented that after three years in captivity man becomes more creature than human.

"I remember when I arrived in the El Reno camp, after a year behind the razor wire in LaTuna.

We were woke up at 2:45 a.m., and marched down to R & D. It took the guards two hours to make sure we had nothing on us to take to another prison (cloths off, spread your ass, stuff like that). Another hour putting on leg irons, belly chains, and hand cuffs.

We were chained together and walked past the razor wire, through the Iron Gate, and outside to the bus. The leg irons allowed for you to step just over a foot at a time, more of a shuffle, than a walk.

As we approached the bus, nine guards with double barrel shotguns held at the ready were watching us. In LaTuna the weather was 88 degrees and very pleasant for the trip to the El Paso Airport.

The days had been windy and warm with a high of 94 yesterday. We were headed for the Holdover Unit at El Reno, Oklahoma. The metal digging into my wrists and ankles were unpleasant the first hour, and completely unbearable after that.

Breakfast and lunch, on the airplane, were a brown paper sack with a slice of salami, two pieces of bread, a half-pint of milk, and one small apple. To eat requires your mouth going down to the food. The handcuffs kept your wrists attached to your belly chain, which is chained to the leg irons around your ankles. My six-foot body had about four-foot of chain, effectively keeping me from being able to set or walk in an upright position. This is all part of the punishment for being a bad man.

I overheard the U.S. Marshall's in the next seats up from me say: "These Negroes are made for this shit, man. They are too lazy to find real work, so; they get caught selling drugs and come in here to lay up for a while. They take to this crap like little ducks to water."

Three hours on these chains and your back keeps you from thinking so much about the circulation being cut off in our feet and hands. In five hours the steel has worked it way into the bone and blood begins dripping from your wrists and ankles.

Thankfully, God makes you numb to anymore pain and you go into a kind of coma-shock. I figure its because Man has no limit to the amount of suffering he wants to see, but God does.

"ConAir" lands in Austin, Texas, and a prisoner who wanted his heart medicine (nito tabs) with him on the trip protested a little too much back in LaTuna, and is taken off so the U.S. Marshals can beat up on him without the rest of us witnesses it.

We land in Houston to take in more prisoners. Some of the inmates from LaTuna are going to the Federal Prison near Houston, but all prisoners were required to go through the Federal Holdover Unit in El Reno, Oklahoma. These Houston Prisoners will be brought back by Bus (and have another nightmare from hell).

Finally, ConAir arrived at their special hanger at Oklahoma City Will Rogers Airport. The Prison Busses are waiting. It's 4:30 p.m. the temperature is 21 degrees with a 26-mile per hour wind out of the NW.

The air is thick with tiny pieces of ice (it is too cold to snow). Scooting down the ramp in back of the plane wearing only a T-shirt, thin khaki pants, and no underwear, was so disconnected my mind would not add up what was going on.

"God, please take all the bad thing I ever done and if I deserve this kind of punishment, just strike me dead right now, please, please, please."

Why did I want to help those people make money in the Stock Market? Why did I want to help them save on their Taxes? Why didn't the Investment Company succeed? WHY didn't I keep my big nose to myself? WHY? WHY? WHY?

The other guys look so pitiful. You can feel there suffering, but it just was not you in this picture, was it?

Before you get to the bus (with no heater), your body refused to move any further and you fall down on the black asphalt. One of the U.S. Marshal's helped me get on the bus (most of them are nice human beings it's the few ugly ones that make them all look bad).

The trip to El Reno takes about 20-25 minutes. I am in no better shape trying to get off the bus than I was getting on it.

"Off the fucking bus, you pussy wimp." WHAM—he hits me hard as he can on the side of the head just above my left eye. WHAM - he popped me again high in the middle of my back with his number 12 boot. This U.S. Marshall's eyes are glazed over with the power he is receiving from this domination of another person. He garbs me by my belly chain... pulled me up...and dragged me down the aisle...to the door as fast as he can move...and shoved me out of the Bus from two steps up.

Without being able to move my arms more than a foot away from my body, I did a belly flopped on the ice covered prison driveway.

I woke up inside FCI El Reno R & D. My skin stings like fire as it begins to warm up from being frozen. The first thing I think is that I am not dead.

Two large cages were crammed full of inmates. Each cage was made to hold one hundred and twenty people. At this time they were holding four hundred each. The prison guards were processing five prisoners at a time.

An inmate would get up on a step latter and the guard would remove the leg Irons, belly chain, and handcuffs. The inmate would remove his cloths and the guard would have him hold up his arms and turn his hands around bend over and spread it, turn around and hold up your cods. Lean your head toward the guard and open your mouth wide.

"Lean over further and shake your hair with your hands. Put these clothes on and move inside."

Inside the office staff completed records and medical people brought your file up to date.

Then, you would be placed in another steel cage to wait for the others to be processed.

Another brown paper sack with a slice of bologna, two slices of bread, mustard, half-pint of milk, and a small apple, was handed out.

I sat in the cage next to the outside window. I could see a group of Cubans were waiting to come in. Ice covered these prisoners, and the ground. Fifty human beings standing in two twenty-five man rows between the outside and inside razor wire. They had on the same kind of thin tee shirt and khaki pants as mine. It is a little colder than when I arrived in Oklahoma City, but from the way the sleet was coming down to the ground I could tell the wind seems to have died down some. Sheets of Ice still blotted out the light making these poor Cubans seem to vanish then reappear.

I see four U.S. Marshals wearing foul weather gear walking up and down the two lines of former human beings. There seems to be no movement from the Cubans, but the captors are hitting and kicking them anyway. Sorry Bastard's wanted to find freedom in the U.S. they deserve this shit, right?

How long had I been inside and how long had they been freezing to death, out there, I really can't say. Just for the time I watched them they had to be frozen solid. It was after eight O'clock in the evening, and everything you see is so bleak you wonder what has happened to humanity. Have we become so inhuman and evil that we enjoy seeing this kind of suffering?

Our group was finally worked through to the inside. The Cuban's were marched in, single file. I noticed some were likely over 65 years old and one could not be over 16. A lesser person would have been completely defeated. These frozen Cubans must be used to this kind of treatment. Even the old guys had a defiant look about them (like you may kick my butt around but my spirit lives on - praise the Lord.).

As I was moved in with the others I noticed a pile of dark blue Navy p-coats stacked in the supply room. Must have been more than a hundred of them just stacked up nice and neat!

At 11:25 p.m., I walked down a hall leading to the front tower. A tired prison guard with no gun walked beside me.

"Coming through," the guard yelled up to the man in the tower. "Got a new Camper here."

The heavy metal door popped as the electrically controlled bolt snapped back. We went through the first gate covered with razor wire, then the second gate.

Lord, here I stand, on the outside. For the first time in nearly two-year's I was outside looking back at the razor wire with no chains on my feet, wrists, or belly.

The Guard pointed to a concrete block building five hundred feet west of the Guard Tower and said, "go over there and find Officer Buntrock, tell him you just came on ConAir from LaTuna FCI."

Tears welled up in my eyes as I crossed the street and parking lot to FPC El Reno. The guard got in his car and headed for Route 66.

One minute I am fucking Al Capone, and the next I am on a public street with no guard and no handcuffs.

It was the first time I could measure the pressure I had been gathering during my time behind the prison walls. In the middle of the night, thirteen and one-half years are remaining on my sentence. No guards around, that I could see, anyway. How many nights had I dreamed of escaping? Building a huge kite and sailing over the wall or cutting a hole in the wire. It was my favorite thing to do when the horrors of prison life were too much for an innocent person to take. That and dreaming about my younger days on Lees Creek. It was just too painful to think about home and family. It would make me worry too much about whether they were all right or not.

From where I had been to this kind of freedom, in less time than it took to walk a block, caused me to set down on the curb in the middle of this freezing ice storm. The block from the tower to the camp seemed more like five or six.

It was two miles from the prison to downtown El Reno. The first few trips I made as the camp "town driver" it seemed like I would never get where I was going. For a year my world was a quarter of a mile in any direction. The first few times I drove the 20 miles to Oklahoma City it seemed was like going from Ft. Smith to Little Rock. Like, I thought I was never gonna get there. After a couple of weeks it was a normal 20-mile trip.

Officer Buntrock is an old guy maybe 65 or 66. He is big with a deep voice and a weird since of humor. Some days he comes into your cell and dumps everything in your locker onto the middle of the floor and yells…"pick it up home-town." The next day he might talk about flying his airplane.

21

"So, what's it like out there in the real world?" Sparks asked.

Robert Lee Sparks is a tall, skinny, kid of a man that is too white with too many red freckles. He is in his early twenties. His mother's family was from the south, and Sparks had never met his daddy or knew anything about him. Robert Lee was born in Plano, Texas. A red hared, freckle faced kid who would always be skinny. His eyes gave the impression that he knew a little more then he was going to ever tell.

The reason he is in the Federal Prison System changed as much as his mood, but mostly he says "drugs". He got me to file his 2255(post-conviction appeal) and I know he pled guilty to changing the speedometer reading on a car he was selling. I asked why he wanted everyone to think he was into drugs? He said, "I don't want nobody to think I did a sissy thing like running a couple thousand miles of my car and got caught."

"What's it like in the real world" I repeated his question. "Hard to explain. I begin. It was nice seeing the Old Capital Building again. It brought back a lot of memories of my first life. Like a dream that is opening up for real.

When the traffic on Lincoln Blvd., in Oklahoma City, allowed me a chance to look up ahead. There was the State Capital, my mind said no way you were ever there. I got this picture of someone who had reached the top of the power pole, but that person wasn't me. Someone with a pretty wife, two great kids, and three grand children.

Twenty years ago, I looked like that guy all right, but I am only dreaming. It never really happened. I am with three or four hundred convicted felons in the Federal Prison Camp and there are two thousand more behind the razor wire in a Federal Correction Institution at El Reno. Some are guilty and some are not guilty, ninety-nine percent are poor, and none of them are happy.

After three years behind bars, I begin to notice that I could tell the difference between the innocent and the guilty. Like a dog that has been trained to smell drugs at the bus stations and airports. I can almost tell by the way he breaths if he has received "*Poor Justice.*" The guilty have an attitude something like "I did the crime and I'm doing the time, just leave me alone."

The innocent goes around looking for another inmate to tell what happened to them. Like they are going to find someone who can correct this horrible mistake.

"Why am I here? Somebody got me! What happened, man? Please help me catch a break!!! Yes, its me, I have been screwed, the government has screwed me."

I have offered Governor Keating the opportunity to use my talent to find and remove those innocent people in the

Oklahoma Prison System, but so far he wants them to stay behind bars.

Would you believe I kept Willy Sparkman from killing Frank Keating when we were in the Oklahoma Legislature, and today I cannot even get a hello out of him?

Yes, Virginia, there are innocent people in prison. And, yes there have been many poor defenseless people executed in Oklahoma and Texas.

Poor old Charley Foster got his "*Poor Justice*" last year. Oklahoma put a needle in his arm and killed him. Not only was he not guilty, Mr. Foster only had the mind of a 9-year-old child.

He stood outside a store for half an hour. Waiting for his wife to pick him up. The two of them went to her folk's home in Texas in a car she borrowed from the victim. Some of her folks were sick and she had to get down there and see them.

I voted for the death penalty to be reinstated in Oklahoma in 1976. I supported it and talked other Legislators into voting for it. The idea was for it to be there as a deterrent, Not for us to should actually execute anyone.

I know now it is no deterrent and bad evidence is presented in some trials. Honest people withhold evidence in order to gain a conviction.

The least we could do is have a committee of non-lawyers oversee the Justice System and spend a little money on those found to have gotten the low end of the stick. What I am saying is that I think they should, at least, be guilty first. For every hundred poor person executed there should be one rich person. No more than three killings a year in Oklahoma, and no more than ten in Texas. How about this? Of the seven hundred on death row pick out the fifty most deserving and put them to sleep.

I figure the same law that put me in prison for fifteen years on three counts of fraud should put Cleta Dethridge Mitchell's husband in the same amount of time. Dale was convicted on ten counts of fraud, got ZERO time. As in NONE. How fair is that? Just because Cleta changed to a Republican and they have a lot of money?

Or, that the same Federal Judge who gave me 15 years for a first time conviction involving $32,800 dollars should give "Tink" Wilkerson more than fifteen months for many more counts involving more than 3.5 million dollars.

I would never vote for the Death Penalty again, knowing the kind of unequal Justice this Country is dispensing. Not just poor people, but Blacks and Mexicans are treated different. In my case it was political pay back. I want to take my vote back.

22

"Lock down, Lock down, go to your cells. Let's go… Let's go… Move it...shitheads."

Officer Buntrock was standing in the door yelling like crazy. A loud alarm was ZIIPing, ZIIPing, ZIIP'ing. Inmates begin walking slower than before.

Other Hacks were yelling and waving their hands for the prisoners to get asses in gear. "Step it up. Let's go girls." The HACKS were shouting.

"What's up?" I asked Robert Lee Sparks, as I reached 110 First Street (our Cubical).

Bobby Rogers stuck his head out of 111 First Street (the Cubical across the hall from us) "Bear's escaped. It's old Bear, he's fucking escaped." He said.

Rogers once worked in the kitchen. His hustle was stealing food and selling it to other inmates. It was mostly fruit, onions, tomatoes, bake goods, and sometimes even real meat. When we had fruit or baked goods on the menu we were only allowed one piece and had to eat it before leaving the cafeteria. Us bad boys were never allowed to have an onion or a whole tomato.

Inmate's either have access to lots of money from the outside, or they to have to hustle. The prison pays 15 to 25 cents per hour for working six hour a day, five day a week. The Dairy pays 15 cents an hour for a five-hour day, six days a week (three shifts).

You can have up to $20.00 in quarters for the pop, candy, and popcorn machines. So, for money in excess of the limit, we either use cigarettes or postage stamps. A female hack charges fifty bucks for a lay. She is a well-built blond Norwegian looking woman from Minnesota. Stacked well enough to need help carrying out all the quarters she earned each night.

Sometimes your job determines your hustle, and sometimes you have to purchase it. Two guys clean and wax each room on First Street and the inmates pay them $1.00 per room each week, or 25 cents from each person in a room (if its full). They must be able to get access to the buffer and wax. And, to do the work after everyone goes to work at 8:00 a.m. and complete all the rooms before the rooms are inspected at 10:30 a.m. The cripples usually do this job.

Before I got access to an electric typewriter, I was one of the two people who cleaned up the twenty rooms on First Street. I paid $50.00 dollars to the previous cleaning person, and received the same amount when I begin typing legal briefs for a dollar per page.

When I got a real job as the Town Driver, I had to work the hustle at odd hours. Several times I went down in Texas to pickup a Dairy Driver whose truck had broken down. Mostly

I went into town to pickup supplies for the main prison, and carry prisoners to and from the bus station or airport. Prisoners on furlough could fly in and out.

Jimmy "Bear" Snow is a short, heavy built, long hared twenty-six year old. He has a dark bushy beard that makes him looks like a bear. He is in prison for running drugs for the Fed's.

"Hell he just got here." Sparks said.

I said, "Two weeks ago, today I believe."

"They found his weed eater still running and the crew truck gone" Rogers said. The hack that runs the landscape crews checks on his men all the time, but only counts them in at 8:00 am and out at 3:30 p.m.

"He had last seen Bear at around 2 p.m., and that was about an hour ago." Rogers added.

"How do you know it's Bear." I asked.

"I was in Crawford's office when the Hack came and reported it" Rogers replied (Mr. Crawford is the Camp Administrator)

Old Lyle and Leo Kingston join us in the hall between our cell and Rogers. Lyle Gordon is a skinny little sixty-year-old man from Ft. Worth. He was once a mechanic for a famous race car driver (according to him). The Fed's caught old Lyle running drugs. To get himself a lighter sentence, Lyle setup his supplier (his own brother). His five-year sentence was reduced to months, and he went home in 12.

After Lyle's van was loaded with power, called cocaine, the Fed's moved in and arrested two boys from Mexico and Lyle's brother.

The Judge gave the Mexicans 30 years each. Lyle's brother hired Race Horse Haynes and got off (something about illegal search, entrapment, or something).

The word was out that anyone who knocks off Lyle cold receives one hundred dollars worth of stamps. And, someone on the outside would hand a friend ten thousand dollars green money.

I thought about putting a sign at the foot of my bed with my name on it. Didn't want anyone coming in the middle of the night and get the wrong old man.

Leo was a Former State Senator from Northwest Oklahoma City. He and his wife, Paulette, were found guilty of HUD Fraud. They fixed up HUD homes and sold them. Leo believed what they were doing was legal. From what I could see of his case, anyone could have made the same mistake.

Leo and his wife are costing the taxpayers $60,000 per year for three years. That is more of a crime than what they done are.

"A chopper picked Bear up out at the cemetery" Leo said, as he walked in.

"How do you know?" Rogers asked.

"Man, cause I was there" Leo replied

"Where?" Sparks asked.

"Fort Reno" Leo answered.

Leo works for the dairy and they were over on "Indian Land" loading Hay.

Lyle works at the dairy office. These guys are hauled back and forth in a van. It's about two miles out to the farm/dairy.

Sparks works in the laundry. You put your washing in a string bag with your tag on it. Sparks put all the bags in a large commercial washer, dryer, and permanently wrinkles everything.

His hustle is to take your clothes out of the string bag and wash them in a regular washing machine. While the cloths are still hot, Sparks folds them. He can't Iron or starch anything because they're eight other inmates earning money for that service.

Other hustles include getting extra feathers sewed inside your pillow, a cotton blanket, better made clothing, new underwear, shaving cream, lotions, and cooked food.

Regular prison food is bad. Hamburgers are made from soybeans or something non-meat and the fish they usually serve on Friday tastes like cardboard and smells like shit.

Each street has it own bookie, bootlegger. With some actual legal experience, my locker is always full of chips, dips, and soda pops.

Ninety-nine per cent (99%) of those I met during my five years in prison admitted they are guilty. Some of the guilty people believed they got a raw deal in the amount of time they received compared to people with money that did the same exact crime.

I filed 804 applications for reduction of sentences (U.S.C. Sec.2255). 31 received some kind of relief. One man got immediate release after seven years in prison with three more years to go. He was happy enough to give me be his fan and cotton blanket, when he mustered out.

Another inmate received an 18-month reduction, but most were of the six months to a year. One man who got nothing from my litigation, but received relief later—Five years ago, he made a deal with the government (he would pled guilty and testify against the other's involved in the drug operation, in return -his sentence would be three-year). I could never get the Federal Trial Judge, in North Carolina, too reconsider the twelve-year sentence he imposed.

Later, the convict's wife and children were traveling down I-40, when a load of Guardrail fell off a semi-trailer on top of their car. The wife was badly hurt and spent seven days in the hospital. As part of his deal, the personal injury Attorney would go to North Carolina and get a new hearing on his sentence. Two weeks after the Attorney returned to Oklahoma, the inmate was signing his release papers.

It's a shame, in so many cases, I found money determined the amount of justice or injustice these inmates received. In at least ninety of those cases where no relief was granted, I believe with access to the courthouse and $10,000 I could have received significant time reductions for 80-90 others inmates. Each inmate costs the taxpayers $25,000 to $30,000 dollars per year, so, for the taxpayer, it would be money well spent.

"I saw this chopper landing over at the cemetery. We stopped loading hay and drove over there. Two guys jump out of the Landscape truck and get in the chopper. Last I seen the chopper was disappearing off to the south." Leo said

I said, "There was two of em, who was the other guy?"

"It was that Colombian guy that came in with Bear" Leo said.

"Shit, I bet it's a fucking Federal Chopper." Sparks said. (Sparks had a lot of conspiracy theories. Some even involved the FBI/DEA killing people).

The only confirmation I received of anything that drastic was Rusty's dad. He was hauling drugs from South America for the CIA. He is missing, and Rusty thinks the CIA did it.

"That would be El Correcto, you know how the Fed's work." Rogers replied.

At the end of the hall were three Prison Officials with a roster. They are going to make a picture count. (A requirement when there is an escape).

I said, "everyone better look like their picture and remember their Federal ID number, otherwise you go to the Hole"(special housing unit—SHU).

"Hole my ass, its proper name is "shoe" Rogers said as he holds his little finger up like a tea sipper.

I said, "Give me a break, ain't nothing special about the hole, except how cruel it is."

"Bear" and the other guy sold drugs for the Federal Government. An outside agency caught them, so, the U.S. Attorney had to charge and convict them. Two weeks after they to prison the FBI gets them out. Likely they are back at work entrapping some other poor person who needs money bad enough to break the law. Is this a great Country or what?

23

The El Reno FPC was built outside El Reno FCI for the purpose of holding Oklahoma County Commissioners who broke the Federal Law.

There are seventy-seven counties in Oklahoma with three Commissioners in each. The commissioners were guilty of taking a 10% kick back from suppliers. The commissioner, R.C. Williams, from my hometown, Sallisaw, used the 10% to open graves for families in his district. He paid people to drive folks to a Hospital, sometimes as far away as Houston. He would pay for driveway culverts out of this money for anyone in his district that needed a new one.

Of the past and present county commissioners that I had contact with only one refused to take the money, and everyone in every county knew it was going on. The Corrugated Metal

Pipe Manufacturers had three prices: Contractors, Wholesalers, and Public.

RC could call Southwest Factories, Inc., where I was a sales-man-(today-Dub Ross Pipe Company). I would price 18"- 16 gage pipe was $3.40 per foot. He would call Henry Peak in Muskogee and get a quote of $3.40 per foot and 10% cash refund. I would sell Mr. Peak's company the pipe at the whole-sale prices of $2.60.

Henry Peak went to prison the week following dedication of "Henry Peak Boulevard" in Muskogee, Oklahoma. Henry was making a living doing what everyone had been doing before statehood. I really liked Henry he was a fine man.

I was happy R.C. was out of office when the Fed's made the decision to prosecute these old politicians. A hundred and sixty-two Commissioners went to the newly built Federal Prison Camp in El Reno, Oklahoma, along with their Suppliers. I always wondered how Dub Ross got off he was one of the dealers.

After I quit Dub Ross, I went to work for Virgil Perry at Midwest Supply. In addition to Manufacturing Corrugated Metal Pipe, Perry sold bridge beams and other road building material as Perry Tire and Supply. Mr. Perry received a pretty stiff sentence. He was a nice person and to old for prison time.

There was only One County Commissioner who refused the 10% deal (that I ran across) that was in Nowata County. I always thought that man deserved a monument built for him.

The camp is divided into halls called Streets (First, Second, Third, and Fourth). I am in the middle of First Street and my cell number is 110. Each street has twenty cells holding four prisoners each.

"First and Second Street" shares one bathroom with eight sinks, four stools, and two pissers. Across the hall from the bathroom is a room with six open shower stalls, no curtains and no doors.

On "Main Street" are two counselor rooms, law library, and six pay phones on the left. And, on the right, a supply room, TV room, and a recreation room. At the end of "Main Street" is the bathroom and showers for the inmates living on "Third and Fourth Streets."

On "Front Street" there are the cafeteria, visiting room, two more counselors' rooms, church, education room, and medical and dental rooms. In the middle of all these streets is the HACKS (Horrible Asshole Carrying Keys) Office.

It all worked fine when there was only one county commissioner (prisoner) per room. When the Prison added three more beds, lockers, people, and overload became the order of the day.

In the mornings there is always a long line formed to use the stools, and the showers. Sewer lines backed up in the stool and ran down the streets on a semi-monthly basis. The smell was something to write your Judge about (i.e. cruel and unusual punishment).

Robert Lee Sparks, Leo Kingston, Lyle Gordon, and I, share one 8x10 room with a double window over looking the visitor's playground. I don't know why but this unsanitary stuff reminds me of a rhyme I heard at Oklahoma University. There was a young man from Boston who drove around in his Austin, there was room for his ass and a gallon of gas, but his ball hung out and he lost em." We had room for a toothbrush, razor, comb, and our ass, but not much else.

Sparks mother, Dottie Lee Sparks, claims to be related to the great civil war General Robert E. Lee. Dottie brings the three little kids up to visit their father (Dottie Lee's "sonny boy.") every Sunday.

"Hell, man, I been locked up in this shit hole for two damn years, why would I give a good goddamn about the capital of Oklahoma?" Robert Lee Sparks brings me back to the moment.

"What's it's like driving down a real street, seeing people on the outside? Do the people you pick stuff up from know you're a fucking prisoner like me?" Sparks asked.

I said, "I tell you I drove by the Capitol, and you're asking me what it's like, right?"

"No, no, shit no man, you and Leo can talk about your fucking glory days at the capital, the guy that was locked up for twenty-four years. Tell me some more about that poor son of a bitch."

"You mean Jordan, the old guy with the MJ Smile?"

"Yes, that guy, how bad did he look after twenty-four years in the joint? What was he in for?"

I said, "He had that dead man prison gray color, like dead people without makeup. The Fed's gave him a bus ticket to New Orleans, a new pair of pants, shirt, jacket (not lined), and a new pair of cardboard shoes (black). He had his discharge papers in one hand, $2,040.00 check in the other (payment for twenty-four years of welding for Unicor), and a small plastic bag between his knees." His eyes flickered in out of focus, like his lights were going on and off. The way they darted around kind of reminded me of a kid doing something bad and was afraid he was about to get caught. Every few seconds a tremor would begin in his hands and feet and move up and down his body, causing his head shake like he was having a small stroke.

I had put a medium sized box with the stuff he accumulated over the past twenty-four years, in back. It might have weighed 50 lb.—Which would make it about two pounds per year.

When I picked Jordan up at the R&D Gate, the HACK said "Take him by the bank, he's gonna need some cash."

We went through the First Union Bank drive-in window. It took the old prisoner, with the MJ smile, several extra seconds to put the discharge papers down and sign the check. Getting it all picked up and put away in it's proper place, was something the old guy was attempting to do, when we arrived at the El Reno bus station. I got out, grabbed the box out of the back and started inside.

I stopped and waited for him, then went to open his door. "Please"…he said, "just let me set here a while, Okay?"

Clearly, this guy was under more pressure than his system could handle. Little tremors moved his large muscles, and his hands went back and forth from the envelope to the cash and little bag.

"I was fine till they closed the big gate." Jordan managed to squeeze out through his clenched teeth. Finally, Jordan rolled his knees out the truck door and hunched his big body forward. Was he getting out or gonna throw up? "The real world gonna take more than I got." He stammered.

I said, "Just calm down, let all this stuff comes to you, you're pushing to hard or something. Hell, I got all day, we damm sure ain't in no hurry.

Everyone I bring up here that's been down more than five years has something like this going on in his mind. Their thinking brain has been out of order for so long it will take a few days for it to get up to speed. For twenty-four years the planning ahead part of his brain had mostly been on vacation while the rest of his brain in on auto pilot (eating, blinking, breathing, welding, talking and walking a person can just do those things without thinking or remembering he did them).

What to fix for lunch, how much of it is in the icebox, what will you need to get at the store, have you got enough money to get it. Where am I going tomorrow. How do I get my kids to behave. How do I impress the boss and get a raise. All takes thinking.

"You ever been driving and not remember part of the trip?" I asked Sparks.

"Oh yeah, I've done that" He replied.

After all this time, his brain was being asked to plan ahead and take care of present business at the same time. He was catching a bus to New Orleans.

His son was twenty-seven years old and a graduate of Tulane University (an eye surgeon) would be waiting at the bus terminal. He wanted to come to El Reno, Oklahoma, and get his dad, but the Fed's considered a person traveling from a prison to a half-way house as "In Custody" and you travel the way they say (Which will never be the most convenient for the prisoner or his family).

His Wife had remarried, but continued to live with her new husband in Jordan's family home, in the old part of New Orleans.

His daughter, Annie Mae, was four when he was put in the joint. Seven years later, she went missing and has never been found.

"She will be Twenty-eight on the thirteenth of next month. I know she's alive - somewhere. I'm gonna find her and when I do, my life will end up having some meaning again." Jordan said.

"Jesus man you hear all that on a four mile trip to the bus station?" Sparks interrupted.

"It's nerves, I think. Jordan talked all the time. To me, himself, his son, his ex-wife, his lost daughter, who knows, he kept going in one form or another the entire time we were going up to the Bus Station.

He told me about being a fullback for Jackson State, before he and his brother robbed that bank."

"The Big old two hundred-fifty pound man just set there looking at his two hands and the three things he had to carry into the bus station?" Sparks asked

"Right, he moved the envelope with the release papers in it and the envelope with the money, back and froth from one hand to the other, all the time giving the bag between his legs a terrified look. Finally, he put down the money envelope and picked up the bag.

"Will you carry the money for me?" he asked.

I already had his box, so, I pickup the money, and he followed me to the ticket window.

The ticket lady stamped his ticket, gave him his part of it, put a tag on his box, and carried it to the back room for the Bus Driver to pickup.

As she went out of sight, the old black man with the pale gray face and wonderful MJ smile looked sick again.

"I can't make it, man. It's just too much, you understand what I'm saying, take me back, man, I can't make it'? He said, as tears rolled down in his face.

"I can only imagine, Guy. I've felt some of this shit, but nothing like what you are going through. How are you gonna find your daughter if you rot in prison?"

He went down on both knees, put his huge hands flat down on the floor and looked up at me. "I can't make It." he repeated. "I should be at work, I been down too long. I can't see what I should be doing next, my mind is gone wild. I can't make it stop spinning."

To those in the bus station/fast food store he was strange looking and they begin to come in for a closer look. MJ wiped the tears away and waited for me to tell him I would take him back.

Several people came over and asked, "what's up with that guy?"

I said, "He's lost his four year old daughter and is worried about finding her." Most of them offered to help look for her. I told them he lost her a while back, but thanked them for the offer.

I threw my chest out and took a deep breath. Using my impression of Officer Buntrock, which is a cross between John Wayne and Ward Bond.

I said "Look hometown, I got your can't, motherfucking, make it right here (I grabbed by right hand between my legs) I'm so damn sorry for your motherfucking ass. Your little Federal vacation is over and now you gonna have to put your fat old black ass back to work in the real world. Boo Hoo, ain't it just too bad that your gonna get a chance to watch you grand kids grow up? You is gonna do it, and you is gonna do it right now, so; shut the fuck up and get your sorry old ass in gear. You hear me?"

The bus pulled in as I was shaking my fist at this giant of a man. "There is the bus and your damm sure getting on it Hometown?"

His big brown eyes were fixed on me and he was very still. In a much lower voice I said "Listen up bud, it will be two days before you even get to New Orleans, when you get there tell your son he's gotta check you into the halfway house and ask him to wait for you to get a pass. You understand home-boy? That's all you gotta think about for two whole days?" His eyes seemed to brighten a bit and I am beginning to be pleased with myself.

I knew this was more like what he was used to hearing for the last twenty-four years. I put my hand on his broad left shoulder and finished my pep talk. "Just slow down, you have no reason for trying to think ahead. The bus driver knows the way to New Orleans he will get there without you doing one single thing but setting. During the next two days you will begin to feel much better and the further you get from the fucking prison, the better you gonna be feeling."

The reward for my efforts came when the MJ Smile filled his whole face, and he said, "I understand that, man, all I gotta do for two days is walk from here to the bus. You gonna walk over there to the bus with me?"

"All right, lets do it." I said. I gave him my future address and phone number.

"When you find your daughter, I want to know about it. Or, if you just want to talk, call me - any time." I said.

"Prison really fucks up your head, man." Sparks whispered. He had tears in his eyes.

I said, "I'll never forget that old guy, but I failed to get his real name. I wish I knew his phone number, I would call him right now.

Maybe he will call me, when I get out."

"You think he would accept a collect call from you?" sparks asked.

Phone calls are the way our Prison System punishes the relatives of Felons. They make a fortune off these; mostly poor families by charging sixty time the going rate for long distance. The money goes to the HACKS for their annual picnic and party. I think the Government should charge a flat fee of $200 dollars for any person who wants to visit one of the criminal bastards. Maybe they should check the financial condition of the family and make them pay the cost of their convict relative.

Seven out of Ten married inmates get a divorce notice within the first year. Two of the remaining three ends their relationship within three years. And, of the ten in a hundred remaining only two will last if the person has more than five years to serve.

It is one horrible sight, watching the little children visiting with their fathers out in the playground. What chance have these poor children got?

One father failed his family, when he received $25,000 dollars from a FBI Agent for drugs he purchased from another FBI Agent for $20,000 dollars. It is really sick to find our Government has played upon the misfortune of the poor to fill the prison system. Most any poor man would take a chance for $5,000, if it didn't involve killing or robbing someone.

I looked at Sparks. I forgot his question.

"Sure your not interested in how it felt to pass by the Oklahoma capital today?" I asked.

"I already told you what you can do with the motherfucking capital." Sparks answered.

"Is that fog or light rain?" Whatever is coming down it's beginning to cover the trees and grass with ice. Only in Oklahoma can you go from Indian Summer to an Ice Forest in one day. I sure hope that old man finds his Daughter.

That night I dreamed of my younger days on Big Lees Creek.

24

The crystal clear water was warm, almost hot, at the surface, but as I dived deeper the cold spring water seemed like ice.

A catfish three-foot long was rushing into a cave near the bottom. I returned to the surface for another breath of air and dove straight for the cave. The channel Cat had turned and was drifting backward into the dark hole. Without seeing him I reached in. The big fish lunged at my hand and swallowed it up to my elbow.

A catfish has thousands of tiny needles for teeth. This 55-pound fish peeled the skin off my arm as I pulled away. My fingers dug into the inside of his mouth and I bought the big fish to the surface.

"Got em or maybe he got me." I yelled to Virgil Denny and Charles Jeremiah.

The big fish splashed and tried to escape, but the bone in his lower mouth is about the size of a baseball bat handle, making it easier for me to hang on to him. I swam to the shallow side of Lees Creek (away from the bluff). Virgil put a rope through the fish's gills and dragged him back to the boat.

I said, " Boy, he get me good."

Charles and his four brothers lived in California for ten years and had moved back to Short, Oklahoma, three years ago. Virgil Denny was thirteen and had never been anywhere else. I am fourteen and I have already been everywhere.

For the last four years I had been back in Short America (where all of our parents were born and raised).

Charles had already seen the blood pouring from my right arm and was running toward me with the First Aid Kit.

"Damn he really got you" Charles said as he poured the hydrogen peroxide all over my right arm.

Big Lees Creek begins at the Devil's Den State Park in Arkansas, runs into Oklahoma for about six miles then back into Arkansas. At around three miles (after entering the State of Oklahoma) are the Big Lees Creek Bridge and a road going East to Uniontown, Arkansas, and West to Nicut, Oklahoma. A hundred yards west of the bridge is the house where my mother, her four sisters, one brother, and I, were born.

This area presently called Short, Oklahoma was previously called Shakespeare. The Postal Service had a hard time delivering mail because no one could spell Shakespeare correctly, so they had to shorten it. The local postmaster suggested Short.

Fifty yards east of Big Lees Creek Bridge is where PaPa Parris operated a general store until high water forced him to move to higher ground. My father, two brothers, and three sisters (one his twin) were all born about ten miles west in Long, Oklahoma. My mother was born in Short, OK, and my daddy was born in Long, OK-this is a true story, I'm not making this up.

Using twelve round logs and six horses PaPa Parris rolled his general store from Long to Short.

In the hot summer, when the creek is at a low level, we use a bow and arrow, or noodle for fish. Most of our time was spent in the old swimming hole. From March to June we would whiz down the stream made double swift by heavy spring rains. Six miles from the Arkansas Line to the Arkansas Line in three flat bottom boats took us four hours. A boy would be on each end of a boat with a girl in the middle. On a really good day we would have two girls in the middle. Half way into the trip, the boys would turn the boats over, and have lots of fun. The girls acted like they were put out with this activity, but they always came back for the next trip.

I was the only boy in the eighth grade at Short. I passed two grades in one year and was the same age as most of the kids in the seventh grade, so it worked out fine. Glena Mae Kelly, *all feed and no belly*, was the only girl in the eighth grade. She was a year older and felt she was too good for a young *kid* like me, so I called her names and was as obnoxious as a Fourteen-year-old could be to a fifteen-year-old girl. Later, we became good friends. When I learned of her death, I cried—remembering some of the things she was a part of up at Short Grade School brought back a lot of other wonderful memories of my days on Lees Creek. Really important things sometimes fail to be recognized and the moment is lost and you have only a memory. As a person gets older the mind allows for a return to the scenes you like best and you can edit in some of the things you wished for years after the event. As time goes by you can actually see this as the real happening. My friends would remind me that I struck out in the big game against Uniontown, but these days I can see the ball soar high into the clear blue country sky and the left fielder racing to catch it. It bounces off his glove for a double and the winning run scores. Being in the highest grade, and the Boy, made me the trail boss in the games we played. Everyone who could be free to play, for the day, was at my house Saturday morning, in time for biscuits and sausage gravy.

Mom usually had two hours work for me before I could go play. Working together we could get it done in twenty minutes. On rainy days we would plan for a boat trip the next day, or, after it quit raining. Then, we would go up to PaPa Parris' big barn full of hay and build forts and stuff like that. We had tunnels going in all directions.

Sometime on rainy days we would build a fire under the bridge and laugh about our past adventures.

Like, the night we camped out at Starr Ford and a big rain forced us to run for higher ground. And, the time we caught Laura Barnes swimming in the raw.

The story we all liked the best was the time two boys from Ft. Smith, Arkansas, pulled upon the gravel bar across from the swimming hole in new red chevy convertible. They swam over to the bluff where we had been playing tag. Without a word, wave, grunt, or anything, one of the boys hooked the tree swing and climbed to the highest part of the rock bluff. He jumped hard to the left to miss the ledge, and went thirty-five feet out over the water and about that high in the air. At the end you either did a flip and dived into the water, or, folded up like a cannon ball and bombed the water. Because from the end the swing returns to the rock ledge with no way for you to miss hitting it. Going backward into the bluff and seeing only the blue sky above takes a professional with guts to just let go without being able to see where you will hit.

The Ft. Smith boy had no guts. He failed to let go and hit the rock ledge hard. Slowly this sixteen or seventeen year old boy slid down the sharp ledge into the water. From the size and looks He was probably a hot shot ball player at Ft. Smith High School.

We named him Tarzan, and his buddy, James. They slowly swam back across the creek, mostly dog paddling, leaving a trail of blood. Not a word was said, nothing from start to finish.

Tarzan and James got back in their fine red automobile, with the top down, and drove off into the sunset.

The Tarzan story generally brings us around to the adventure of Mr. Reeder. Old man Reeder and his lovely wife, Mary Bee, crossed Lees Creek at the ford about a hundred yards below the swimming hole. Mary Kay was shocked at seeing six boys swinging off the rock bluff with their "pee pee's" swinging in the breeze.

Mrs. Reeder came by the house and told my mother she saw her son's "pee pee." Momma told her it was no big deal, she had seen it a few times herself.

"You allow your boy to go around like that?" Mary Bee asked

"No, he pretty much does that on his own." Momma said.

Mr. Reeder went out the to swimming hole, climbed up in the tree, and cut the cable down.

The next morning, we found his flat bottom metal boat and shot it several times with our rifles. It sank slowly to the bottom in ten foot of water. You might say this boat was DIC. (Dead in Creek).

We went to PaPa Parris' store and purchased a new rope with some of our strawberries picking money. Stilwell, the strawberry capital of the world, is ten miles north of Short.

We got the new swing up just in time to take a hot afternoon swim before I had to go home and feed PaPa Parris' horse, Penny, and milk the cow.

I got chewed out for not weeding the garden for mom. Dad eats more of the food from the garden, than anyone else, so, why was sit mom's garden?

Two days later, Mr. Reeder climbed the tree and cut the new swing down.

The next Sunday, we harvested Mr. Reeder's watermelons for him. While he and his lovely wife, were at the Seabolt Church over at Belfonte, we picked over five hundred large black diamond melons and threw them in Big Lees creek. Then, we went downstream to the swimming hole and waited for the melons to float to us.

It took almost two hours to bust them open and eat the hearts out. Somehow the word had gotten out, and kids from as far away as Van Buren, Natural Dam, Figure Five, Bell, and Cedarville showed up at the swimming hole to help us with the dirty job of eating the melons. It was 95 degrees in the shade but those melons had cooled out good in the spring fed creek water.

We put up another swing while we were enjoying ourselves.

The next morning, Mr. Reeder came by the store, without Mary Bee. He told PaPa Parris about his trouble with some vandals.

Mr. Reader kept looking at me the whole time, making certain I was listening when he said:

"That's it, I will never bother those kids swimming hole again."

"What Kids swimming hole? I thought you were talking about a boat and your crop of melons?" PaPa Parris asked.

"Not sure how they connect. Mr. Reeder said, just wanted you to know if you hear anything about the boys that might have done some things over in the back pasture, and—will, I just would appreciate it if you could pass the message along for me? Mr. Reeder asked.

"Fine with me. Don't mind getting the word around for you." PaPa Parris said.

Mr. Reeder looked at me and waited for a few seconds. I gave them a little up and down nod, and he walked out the door.

Mr. Reeder was a good neighbor after that, even purchased a few baseballs for the Short ball club (Red Birds).

"What about the time we whooped those Stilwell Indians?" Virgil asked to get the story started. As usual, everyone took part in telling about the time we won the Baseball Tournament at Stilwell. (Actually the older guys won, but we were there, and did our part).

Stilwell invited the Short "Red Birds" to their baseball tournament and put us in their bracket. That summer we beat Cherry Tree, North and South Greasy, Maple, Nicut, and Uniontown at home and lost to Marble City, Muldrow, Gans, Central, and Roland away. When Stilwell invited Short to the Tournament, my uncle, H.L.Peace, called Darwin Collins and got him and one of his brothers to join Short for the tournament.

The Brothers had played summer league ball with Muldrow and they were the best around. Stilwell wanted to win their tournament, so they left Muldrow off the invite list.

Stilwell never had a chance. Short beat them 9 to 1 in the first game of the double elimination tournament.

Stilwell went out and picked up the best players from all those teams that had been eliminated, but nothing helped. Short won the tournament with Lynn Vann pitching a two hit game.

Sometimes, our stories would get on a winter theme and I would tell about the time I killed twelve quail with one bullet. I started that morning trailing a rabbit. It had came a big snow during the night and the rabbit's tracks were easy to follow. I came across this big rotten log about fifteen feet long, lying on the ground. I noticed a basketball size bundle of brown and black feathers up under the end of the log. One shot into the ball of feathers and thirty quail flew out, leaving twelve behind. I picked them up and went home to clean them for breakfast the next morning.

Twelve quail with one twenty-two bullet is a world record that still stands today. Life was good growing up in Short, Oklahoma.

Dad took a picture of Virgil Denny, Charles Jeremiah, and I, holding up that big old catfish.

Mom put turpentine and sugar on my sliced up arm and wrapped it with stripes she ripped from an old bed sheet.

Fourteen was a great year to remember. In prison you have a lot of time for such things.

"Hey, Sparks, have I told you about the time I killed twelve birds with one 22 bullet?"

25

On April 18, 1995, I drove the prison truck into Oklahoma City and picked up some items for the Dairy. The store was on 5th and Hudson down from the Murray Federal Building. It was nine o'clock when I picked up three items.

When I came out to load the supplies in the bed of the truck, I saw another camper we called "chevy". His real name was Chevrons or something like that. He was a driver for the Dairy. He lived across the hall from me at the Camp. I wondered why I was getting these items for the Dairy, when the Dairy had a man coming to the same part of Oklahoma City.

Chevy was a short, stout built, Mexican man in his early to middle twenties. He always wore dark clothing and a Pittsburgh Pirate ball cap. He was in prison for running drugs from McAllen, Texas to Wheeling, West Virginia.

I went north on a one way street (Harvey or Hudson—I can never remember one from the other). Then I turned back west on Sixth Street. To my surprise there was another Dairy driver. "Jimmy" was just setting there about half-asleep. Jimmy was a tall white boy with short blond hair. His brother was the personal driver for U.S. Senator Dale Bumpers from Arkansas.

Jimmy used a mixture of diesel fuel and ammonium nitrate to blow up an abortion clinic in Arkansas. We all wondered who he "gave up" to only get five years and be able to serve it in a camp. Bombs and guns are considered violent crimes and you do the time behind the razor wire.

When he got the Dairy Drivers Job everyone knew Senator Bumpers had made a call. Six drivers deliver milk to prisons in Kansas, Texas, and Arkansas, in three trucks.

Around two o'clock on April the 18th I went to El Reno to pickup a rebuilt starter. The prison farm's white bulk truck was almost out of sight behind the shop. I pulled around behind the building and found a one ton truck with a 12-foot stakes bed. Fifty-five gallon barrels were being filled with powder from the prison farm truck.

The two men doing the transfer were not anyone I had seen before.

I entered the shop to pickup the rebuilt starter and it wasn't ready.

"Who brought that farm truck in here?" I asked the clerk.

"Chevy" he replied.

"Where is he now?" I asked.

"Gone" he replied.

The camp has fifty or sixty farm hands working the fields from U.S. 66 highway north for twenty miles. Rarely do they get into town. Farm equipment driven by a Dairy worker into the real world (town), would be something a farm driver would die for.

It is something the Farm workers dream about getting to do. When I got back to Camp I looked up Chevy.

I said, "What were you doing downtown."

"Nothing." Chevy said.

I said, "nothing, my ass, what the hell was you doing?

"Me and Jimmy had to take the Dairy Truck in and get it fixed, you never saw us, understand?" Chevy answered.

I said, "There ain't no truck fixing places around NW 5th and Hudson."

"Man, I took the fucking truck to the fucking truck fixing place on Reno and Mac Arthur. Jimmy picked me up and brought me back, period. nobody was on 5th and Hudson, you Understand that?" Chevy said.

I said "Don't shit me, it was you, and Jimmy was around the corner on NW 6th street"

"People with big eyes can fucking die, you know that big shot?" He replied.

I said, "You are so full of shit, you know I have helped twenty people of all colors in here, and thirty more have pending litigation. If you do anything to me, they would make you suffer before killing your ass. Of course, a lock in a sock makes me as young and big as you, so, take it too someone who gives a shit.

"Jimmy, Bobby Rogers, Chevy, and Moss, are in cell no.111, just across the hall from mine. Rogers was caught taking groceries out of the kitchen and his work detail was changed to office manager at the dairy. The dairy caught him selling new farm tires, and nothing happened. I almost went to the hole because transportation was missing a socket. Then, went for tearing up a truck door.

Unexplained things just happen. We buried several brand new computers, still in the box, because someone was coming in for an inspection and if those computers were found the prison would lose a lot of money from next years' budget.

You just learn to go with the flow. Of the entire bizarre, small world, tragic things, to happen in my life, they all combined to take place the next day.

It is April 19,1995, Chevy, Jimmy, and I left the camp at eight o'clock. I went to SW 36th and Meridian and picked up some freight. Then, back to I-40 and headed into Oklahoma City. I turned off I-40 at Western and traveled north two blocks.

I was on my way out to Edmond, Oklahoma, to get a tank for Unicor. At 9:01 a.m. an atomic bomb with off in downtown Oklahoma City, killing 168 people, one Federal Building, the Journal Record Building, the YMCA Building, and damaging many others. A gray cloud with white streaks went up high in the clear morning sky and formed a giant mushroom shape. I had seen those A-bomb tests and this was one.

To this point in History, the greatest act of terrorism in American History is nine blocks from me. The County Jail is three blocks over and from my point of view it looked like the cloud was coming off the top of that building. It was a devastating thing to witness. The day before, at the exactly the same time, I had been down the street.

I turned off Western at 3rd and back west to Villa Street. I drove past my house in Oklahoma City to see if my wife was all right. After the Boom-Boom, and the trimmer, everything was graveyard still. Dogs, birds, bugs, cars, wind, nothing made a sound. People ran out of their homes looking around then back inside to watch what happened on TV. In two minutes I was past my house and on my way to Pennsylvania and 19th Street.

In Oklahoma City NW 6th street is one way west. The bomb went off on NW 5th Street, a one way east. As a person travels west on 6th it begins to curve to the northwest and the name changes Linwood. Linwood runs into Penn., and Penn. goes all the way north to the Edmond road.

I stop at the light at Penn. and NW 19th. The light changes and as I begin to move forward, I saw an old green fords pickup coming from downtown. It was traveling real fast and I could tell it wasn't going to stop for the red light.

The street is a little off center and I figured he just failed to see it until it was too late to stop. The green pickup had a bright blue plastic tarp over the load in the back. It had a Texas Tag and three people were in the cab.

Had I been a regular person, I would have turned south on Penn. and went to help the victims of the bombing. My boss, Dale, might understand, but I couldn't take any chances. Past the light at NW 39th and Penn. and before the expressway exit, the old pickup pulled over on the access road.

The white guy changed places with the, dark skinned driver. From my view he could have been Latino, Asian, Indian, or African. The female in the middle was also dark skinned with long black hair. She looks like "Ruth" from north of Short, Oklahoma. I say to myself, "sure is a small world."

I almost stopped before I remembered what I am. They passed me again around NW 122nd Street.

One corner of the pretty blue trap tore lose as the pickup past the road to Quail Springs Mall. The brakes were applied in a big hurry and both men almost broke their necks getting their load of metal cabinets covered back up.

How many people know the name of the Indians General Custer killed? Or, the Calverymen Chief Setting Bull murdered?

Custer was killed and became a hero. Setting Bull died an old man in a federal prison with no glory.

What will be said of the home grown tragedies of our time on this planet? The Waco and Oklahoma City Horrors we watched in living color, on our TV sets. Cult Kids, Federal Kids, Innocent Adults could have all been saved if the Law Enforcement Agents would have knocked on the door of the Church in Waco and handed them a Subpoena to appear in Federal Court.

Time will have to pass before all the story becomes known. What was going on with that pickup heading out of town? Did they have anything to do with the bombing of the Federal Building? Of all things, for two people from Short, Oklahoma to be going north on Pennsylvania at the same time on the same day must be ten million to one.

Ruthie, what are you doing here? All the vehicles on the road were heading into town, you guys and I are the only ones going out."

I watched the awful thing on TV, all the black smoke and bloody people.

The people loaded my truck with the tank for Unicor and I headed back to El Reno.

I had watched in horror two years before, as the Branch Dividian Compound was burned down. Now, I had seen an even more tragic thing even closer to home.

People in Waco might feel different about which is the most numbing, but everyone will agree, both are beyond words to describe.

The next morning, word went around the camp that the farm was missing 3000 pounds of Ammonia Nitrate. On the second day, we found out that both Chevy and Jimmy were being held for questioning in El Paso. They were in Dallas,

Texas, when Airline tickets were purchased, and three other things that fit.

Chevy looked like the pictures of John Doe #2. And, of course, Jimmy had blown up the Abortion Clinic with Ammonia Nitrate and he was a white boy with short hair like the picture of John Doe #1.

Plus both of them had their pictures on the video cameras downtown.

The Warden fired the Farm Supervisor. He said he used the fertilizer on his personal farm. Three thousand pounds would be a lot for 40 acres. "Okay, he said, I used 1000 pounds and two other guards took the other 2000 pounds."

Guess who John Doe 1 & 2 would have been, had McVeigh not been caught.

26

It turned cold over night and this morning a thick blanket of fog lays across the Federal Correctional Institute at El Reno, Oklahoma. The outside doors are locked when these kinds of conditions exist.

After we finish breakfast each of the four streets (halls) in the camp is bolted shut.

"Lock down, go to your cells" the guard shouts several times. Escape attempts are more common during this kind of weather and the prison camp being outside the razor wire is a concern for the Prison Officials. They worry a camper might give outside aid to the much more dangerous convicts inside.

A "camper" is typically a druggie, white collar lowlife, or, a Citizen of Mexico. They cost the Taxpayers over $25,000 dollars a year to keep away from society. People who commit crimes involving guns or violence are not allowed to serve their time in a Federal Prison Camp. Walking away from a Camp and not being noticed for two hours would be fairly easy. However, if you are silly enough to do it, you would likely be caught and serve the balance of your time behind the razor wire and have an additional three to five years added on to your time.

Six inmates walked off during my five years of criminal service to my Country.

All four of us set on our bunks in that little room with no place to go and nothing to do.

"Remember Jack Simms and his girlfriend?" Leo asked.

His girlfriend would be first to line up in the visiting area. Sometimes she would arrive thirty minutes early just so she would no one would be ahead of her. James would have his visiting cloths on and be at the door.

The second they called his name he was at the visiting desk. Leo got his wife, Paulette, to come out for a visit early one day and discovered the reason girl was so anxious to see James.

Leo was ready and waiting right behind James. The girl checked in and James name was called over the public address system. A minute later Leo's wife checked in and Leo's name was called.

When Leo and Paulette entered the visiting room no one else was there. James and his girlfriend are gone?

Leo says, "in about five minutes James and the girl come out from behind the pop and candy machines that are rowed up along one side of the visiting room." The orderlies who clean up pull the machines out from the wall about three feet. This allows room for a man and woman to get behind them. The Guard has too much to do checking in people at the beginning to make his rounds. We all laugh when Leo finishes telling the story.

When Leo went home I still had a year to go on my sentence. He had entered prison about two months after I arrived from La tuna, and we became friends for a lot of reasons. We hardly ever talked about being in the Legislature, but it was always close on our minds.

The other three hundred "Campers" watched the way Leo was being treated. If it seemed he was getting any slack because he was "a big shot Senator," the guards would hear about it.

Leo worked in the Cow Shit for a year before they lightened up on him. I was older and came in from another prison, without being advertised. The inmates piled up in the halls waiting for the celebrity to arrive.

By the time he left Camp El Reno he had the respect of everyone. He was just a man life the rest of us.

I am going to call the man who took Leo's place in our cell Wayne. He is an easygoing businessman in Oklahoma and might not like to see his name in print. He is the greatest guy in the world.

Tom is the Italian type that all the girls go for. His Girlfriends visit him two or three at a time. Within two weeks he has five hundred arts and crafts magazines stacked up around his bunk.

His ability to make cabinets and whatnots gains him a pickup to drive and on site visits.

Wayne saved some of my stuff when I went to the hole for tearing up the door on the truck.

When a prisoner goes to the hole other inmates break into his locker and steal all of his belongings. Just another way prisoners make doing time harder for other prisoners.

"Parris come to the office." Buntrock says over the intercom. I go to the locked door and the guard opens it from the outside. I could have gone to the other end of the hall and exited through the emergency outside exit all by myself. After a while you just know it's the Government way.

"Go to the airport and pick up a prisoner coming in from California" The Officer Buntrock, said.

I get the keys out of the lock box and go out the back door of the concrete block prison building into a thick, heavy fog. It is past eight o'clock in the morning. What light is available only seems to reflect back into my eyes. I can make out the emergency spotlight at the corner of the Third Street not fifty feet away.

I almost run into a guard with a bulletproof vest and a shotgun standing between the camp and the big prison fence.

Finding my vehicle was more by just knowing where it is than being able to see anything. I am almost ready to unlock the pickup door when there is a sound from the direction of the razor wire twenty feet away out in front of my truck.

The front of my pickup is two foot from the line no camper can cross and I am not about to get any closer to that sound than I am at this moment. I have on a blue shirt and pants (Navy surplus). Behind the razor wire, prisoners ware brown shirts and pants (Army surplus).

"Can you help me" the escapee whispered on the back of my neck.

I jump forward a foot and turned to see The guy that had been standing right behind me. He had thrown a rope over the fence, tied it on the outside, and over he came. All he had to do was keep from getting hung up on the wire.

"Can you help me" he repeated.

"Only to tell you to go back over the fence as fast as you can." I said.

"You're the town driver, are you going into town?" he asked.

"I got a year remaining on my sentence, sorry man. It's two miles to I-40, but don't go that way I pointed to where the guard with the shotgun had been standing." Three steps into the fog and he was gone.

I went to the Will Rogers Airport and picked up a prisoner who had been on a three-day furlough and brought him home. When I got back to the camp, the escapee had already been returned to his cell. Three years will be added to his 30-year sentence.

Should I have said, hunker down in the pickup bed and if I am stopped I don't know you are there? No, I did the right thing.

James Carter was from Eastern Oklahoma. He pled guilty to possession and distribution of a controlled and dangerous substance. His sentence was enhanced by five years because a gun was found in the house where he stayed. A former high school buddy gave him some cocaine. Then, a few days later asked him to pick up a package at Grand Lake, and take it to Dewey, Oklahoma. For helping get this package delivered he would receive one eight ball worth about $250.00. It turned out all three people were DEA Agents. The guy he got the package from, the guy he delivered it too, and the high school buddy he did it for, were just doing their jobs.

James Carter is now gonna cost the taxpayers an additional $100,000 because of the escape attempt.

I had already found out about our government doing stuff like this. At Muskogee, Mr. Glover told me his story. The Fed's purchased a chemical supply company in Tulsa, Oklahoma. For several months, they bought and sold chemicals used in the manufacturing of illegal drugs. Our Government went out and recruited poor people into the business of making and selling their products. Then, after they made Mr. Glover's family wealthy selling dope, they sold him the chemical company and made a huge profit.

A few days later, the Government arrested all of their former customers and now the taxpayers are paying over a million dollars a year to keep them in prison. Seventy-three thousand more people in the Oklahoma, Kansas, Missouri, and Arkansas Area of the U.S. have been exposed to Government provided drugs.

One of the new versions of us should be that our Government never be allowed to manufacture, sell, or recruit others into violating the law. And, we never add time onto a sentence for a gun *not* exhibited or used, or threatened, during the commission of the crime. If we can stop hanging people for singing in church I know we can do this.

27

You hear about everyone in prison being innocent. It's a good reply when someone suggests the law may have made a mistake.

"He said he was innocent".

"Yeah that's what they all say."

The reality of it all is, of the Five Thousand Oklahoma men in federal prisons, across the country in 1996, only one hundred and nine are most likely innocent. Two thousand nine hundred and twenty-one got a stiffer sentence than "Tink" Wilkerson, Dale Mitchell, and Uncle Charles Keating.

That's what pisses off the Oklahoma Men and women who are guilty and in prison.

Uncle Charlie was found guilty on 70 counts of fraud involving eighty million dollars. He could have received 3,500 years. His sentence, by a Federal Judge, was 10 year. My Judge (Seay) could have gave Tink Wilkerson 400 years, but he handed down a reasonable sentence of 15 months. Dale could have received a sentence of 700 years, but Federal Judge (West) gave him Zero time to serve, I could have received 15 years for three counts involving $32,800 and that is how much time I got. Not really fair, even if I had been guilty, I would still be highly urinated. And that's what you hear. Not that they are innocent, its just that the convict failed to receive a fair sentence like "Dale," "Tink," or, "Uncle Keating." The Guy's cooling there heals for something they didn't do, scream loud enough for all five-thousand. Or, maybe "that's what they all say" is a good way to get the public to ignore the Injustice problem.

The "Duck Man" was caught with five dead ducks, 3 miles south of Vian, Oklahoma. He received a three-year Federal prison sentence for killing those five ducks on a Federal Game Refuge. The Duck Man's story is that his duck blind was out in Kerr Lake about four hundred yards from the shore. He says he was in his blind when he killed the five ducks. The Federal Game Ranger arrested him as he was loading his boat on the trailer at Vian landing on Kerr Lake.

The short, fat, little man was actually lucky, the Federal Judge could have enhanced the sentence by five years because it involved a gun. I thought he looked like a little Banta Rooster strutting around acting so innocent and all, but since he killed five ducks, the inmates called him "Duck Man". I had to admit, when he walked with his big butt swinging back and forth above those short little toothpick legs, he reminded me of a duck.

He refused to work and spent a lot of time in the "Special Housing Unit." The Hacks would take him to food service where he would refuse to work and back to the hole he would go for another two weeks.

Four months after I arrived behind the razor wire at LaTuna, the "duck Man" was carried from "SHU" to the prison medical facility. He was covered with blood, his scalp was pealed back and the inside of his brain was exposed.

The Mexican inmate who cleaned up around his cell said he called the big black hack a "nigger motherfucker."

Those hacks that work in SHU put up with a lot of shit. The two weeks I spent in the hole in LaTuna was unforgettable in different ways than in El Reno. It was dark except feeding time, bathing time, and shakedowns. The cells are barely big enough for a metal cot, stool, and wash bowl. The door has a hole big enough for you to back up and stick both hands out into the hall, in order for the hack to put the handcuffs on you before opening the door.

Each day in the hole, Inmates are required to take off all their cloths and walk down the hall to the shower stalls.

A hack sprayed me with soap that smelled like bleach and rotten eggs. I stood under the hot water as long as they let me. Locked in that shower stall was the only place I could believe it was just a spring day back home.

The inmate in the cell next to mine, would get his penis hard and make it jump for the female hacks as he walked down the hall for his shower.

A couple of doors over, was a very large inmate, maybe 350 pounds. He would hold off shitting until his shower time. As the hacks walked him down the hall he squirted it down his legs onto the floor.

His beatings were severe enough to have killed a normal person. I know for sure that I would never have survived those kinds of blows. They would try to beat him into cleaning it up, but he never even went to his knees until he was unconscious.

Other inmate, working the unit, carried the unconscious man back to his cell and cleaned the shit up off the floor. Every now and then, someone would commence screaming the hacks would go in and work him over. Mostly you hear crying, praying and low moaning pain. I figured the screams were from a person who had just lost a little more of his saneness.

The Special Housing Unit in El Reno had two inmates in each cell with upper and lower bunks and a 1/4-inch flat fireproof mattress over the cold steel.

The first thing I noticed was a humming sound like a couple hundred bees out in the hall. When I looked through the 12"x18" hole in the door, I saw white string all up and down the hall. A battery whizzed past by door with string tied to it, and then it begins being pulled into the cell across from me.

He had tired string to an AAA battery and pitched it under his door and down the hall. When the other inmate threw his string and battery over it, the man across from me was able to pull the other man's string and battery into his cell.

A line of communications has now been established, you might say. A cigarette was tired to the line and the man down the hall pulled his way. A sheet of stamps was tired to the line and the man across from me pulled that back to him. This worked great, but the easiest way to pass things around was through the orderlies. As they waxed the hall, they would talk to the prisoners and move stuff.

On commissary day (once a week), the orderlies would bring a cart down the hall to hold all the stuff they had earned by performing these necessary tasks. The guards just looked the other way for all this.

A pouch of tobacco cost $17.00 at the store in town, and orderly would give a $100.00 to a guard for bringing a pouch into prison. He could get in excess or $500.00 for that one pouch of tobacco. Paper, half of a match, small piece of strike pad, and enough tobacco for one roll you're on cigarette cost 20 stamps.

"Where do they get the string and batteries?" I asked my cellmate.

"String from unraveling the sheets, batteries from the commissary" he said.

I went to the hole in El Reno for tearing the door on a fifteen-year-old one ton Dodge prison truck. The wind had caught the door so many times it was more off than on its hinges and it was rusted.

A wicked hack working in transportation named Charlie something stopped me one morning.

"What have you done to this door" he wanted to know.

I said, "you mean this rusty bent up hinge?"

"You did this on purpose." Charley said.

I said, "what are you talking about? The door has had a stick of wood put behind the hinge and sprung back many, many, many times during past ten years.

He wrote me up for damaging the door and I went to the hole for two weeks. I also lost 30 days-good time.

I knew when I got out of the hole I would be assigned to the Dairy and required to shovel shit.

The old truck had been placed on the Salvage list three times, and was more junk than Truck. They now have a new door on and it cost me $386 (a years pay in prison). This would have to be paid before I could go to the halfway house.

Lucky for me, a friend who got out a few months before me was able to loan me the money. Otherwise, I would stay behind bars until the bill is paid. At 15 cents per hour that would have taken a very long time.

The continuous light in the SHU at El Reno caused much of the fighting in the unit. Sometimes new inmates would wet toilet paper and cover the bulbs, shutting off some of the light.

First time the hacks moved the inmates too different cells and tell them "do it again and you will receive a fate worse than death" and laugh.

The second time the inmate would be moved in with "Baby Boy" a two hundred Sixty-eight-pound muscle man that made punks out of his cellmates.

A New guys might think he is pretty smart doing the wet tissue trice, and no one would tell them what was coming until it was too late. Then, as "Baby Boy's" new meat he was lead down to his new room. All the other prisoners would be yelling "fudge, fudge, fudge" and make three kissing sounds over and over again… "Fudge, fudge, fudge, Smack, Smack, Smack." the boys are really having fun, now.

As the guy went by my cell, I could see the terror in his eyes. He realized the wet paper caper had been a very bad idea.

Baby Boy was a 30 to lifer with seventeen down and 13 or more to go. The first time he raped and killed a ten-year old boy and got 10 to 20 years. After only two years in prison he was let out. Three days later he raped and killed another four-teen-year-old boy.

Most of his time is spent in the hole. He actually preferred it in many ways. He had never really liked black boys, or any boy that went around acting prissy like a girl. Baby Boy much pre-ferred the very young Mexican boys, with their macho attitude.

He would never forget the night his homeboy's completely duck taped a young Mexican Boy for him. It is just such a shame they don't put all prisoners in one place. Baby boy would give anything, twice, for a 10-year-old "bad" Mexican boy.

It was such a thrill hearing them scream and try to get away. Of course, he had to kill the young ones. They were his and he could never bare the thought of another man near them.

The man the hacks put in with Baby Boy, (I'll call him "Poor Soul,") screamed for almost twenty minutes, then not a sound of any kind. I prayed for him, and thanked God that I let the bright light keep me awake.

Over two hours passed before the hacks checked on the two lovers in cell A16. Baby Boy was fast asleep he had that well satisfied "look" on his face. Poor Soul was all curled up in a corner naked and cold. Only a near silent sob emerged as tears ran down his face. The shock in his eyes was a permanent thing. It may dim some with time but it will always be part of this man, just as many things in prison remain with people no matter where they go in life. Only a person who has been to hell and back could really comprehend the constant terror inside a Federal Prison.

A day or so later, Poor Soul gave one of the orderlies five books of stamp's in exchange for two combinations locks from the lost property room. Poor Soul didn't care what the combinations were he had other uses for the heavy locks. When he put the "locks in a sock" he had a very formidable weapon.

Poor Soul invented a new way to get in a Federal Prison. He failed to deposit the day's receipts for his employer. The Judge gave him three year's in prison for stealing $13,336 from a federally protected institution.

Poor Soul told the Court he made the deposit in the overnight depository just as he had for the past several years. The Judge becomes so upset and disappointed with the man's lies and taking up the court's valuable time.

"How stupid do you think we are?" the judge asked Poor Soul, before he handed down the sentence.

Federal Judges were handing down one to a hundred year sentences for the same crime. Congress found this unacceptable, and unfair, so, they passed the Sentencing Guideline laws in 1984 and implemented it in 1987. This Judge decided Poor Soul had intended to steal the money at the beginning of his employment in 1986, so, he came under the "old law" of one to one hundred years. Instead of the 1994 guideline sentence of 12 to 14 months, the Judge gave him a three-year sentence.

Poor Soul, was a forty-three year old man with a wife and three kids. They drove up from near Tulsa, Oklahoma every Saturday to see "Daddy". The wife was a nice looking forty-year-old woman, the hacks had fun feeling her up during their search, but they really enjoyed his Fifteen-year-old daughter.

"Daddy, that man stuck his finger inside my panties." The fifteen-year-old told Poor Soul during their last visit.

Fighting with the guards is the reason poor soul was put in the hole."

Late one night, Poor Soul took off his cotton socks, used his hand to run one inside the other. He put the two locks inside the double strength socks, and walked over to where Baby Boy lay on the cot fast asleep.

WHAM. The two locks landed in the middle of baby boy's back. He rolled over and raises his arms to protect his face.

WHACK. The second blow crashed into his right arm seven or eight inches from the wrist down toward Baby Boy's elbow bone was exposed and his hand was just hanging off the end.

WHAM. The third blow cracked Baby Boy's skull and the fourth drove bone chips into Baby Boy's brain. Blood gushed out of the hole, his body jerked, his eyes rolled down then up, he quivered a few minutes but he was already dead.

Sadly, Poor Soul's punishment and abuse would last much longer.

"Get your wife and daughter to meet me at the Best Western Motel out on the Interstate, and I will get you a cell by yourself and make the others leave you along," One Guard promised.

Poor Soul talked to his family, over the phone, once a week, and never again allowed them to visit FCI El Reno.

Almost a year later, the deposit Poor Soul never made along with two other company's deposits that were also missing, were found stuck in behind the overnight deposit mechanism at the bank.

Officials at the bank were very sorry about the error.

For the Federal Government's part, the Judge, and the Prison employees, it was all in a day's work.

"They all say they are innocent, maybe a few really are, its just part of the system. It's the best in the world, but it ain't perfect."

No it is far from perfect. So, I guess we should pass some more laws making it more imperfect?

If a man had a trial it was a fair one. If a man had a lawyer he was a good one. This is the post 1989 mentality of the higher courts.

"Why do these inmates make their folks borrow $2500 or $3000 to hire a lawyer to file an appeal? They are on Food Stamps for god's sake. Don't they know only two in eight hundred cases get any relief?

"Hell, all we can do keep trying."

We're talking two million dollars from eight hundred poor family's welfare checks paid to post conviction lawyers, for possibility of gaining two helpful decisions from the higher courts. The odds are just not good.

It should be a requirement at every law school in this Country for a student to spend one day standing at the phones in a prison. Listening to inmates hassle the wife and kids on the outside.

Every time I went to use a phone, at least, one man would be screaming at someone on the outside. I figured my wife and kids had it worse than I did, and I tried to never call if I was in a bad mood. This is not the normal way things go. It is more like:

"You sell your ass, I don't care, get me some money in here." When I get out, bitch, you better find a motherfucking hole, cause I am gonna rip your motherfucking ass off."

"Get your lazy ass sister to do a little sucking and bucking.

Money, Bitch, send me money, now, or my homeboy is coming for a visit. You got that?"

She works out $3000 dollars so this scumbag can hire a lawyer to file an appeal. The lawyer works two hours, tops, typing up a 2255 motion. He knows at the time he is doing it that the odds are 400 to 1.

It would get the inmate in real trouble, if the person on the outside called in to complain. All the phone calls are recorded. The prison does nothing if there is no complaint. I think the "Homeboy" keeps most everyone in line. Maybe the woman loves this lowlife idiot so much she puts up with his abuse.

When five thousand out of a five thousand and one lost their right to be protected by the Supreme Court, something should have taken their place.

Law Enforcement should only have one voice in who is appointed to Federal Judgeships and the Court of Appeals, not a thousand voices. It seems Prosecutors are promoted over Professors and Defense Attorneys.

We are just as much to blame. Look at how many former Prosecutors are elected to the U. S. Senate and House of Representatives. It is not good that our Court System, Legislature, and Executive Branch are almost completely controlled by Lawyers.

We will never be able to put all the criminals in prison. We can make every effort to keep innocent people out and be fair to all those that are convicted.

No matter how much money you have, the sentence should be the same. The Appeals Court should not attempt to make friends with lower court Judges and lawyers. They should read every appeal and not be thinking about a party they had with a Judge or prosecutor.

I thought about running for the U.S. House of Representatives several years back. I could have received several thousand dollars, "If I would agree to allow a certain group tell me who to recommend be appoint as U.S. Attorney for the Eastern District of Oklahoma."

People, who have missed all the law changes the last ten years, have missed the fact that the U.S. Attorney is the new king of his district. If he is dishonest, look out.

28

It had rained earlier and a heavy cloud was treatening to deliver a real downpour. I was in Oklahoma City picking up microwaves' that had been repaired at a shop over near the State Capital.

The proper way to return to the Federal Prison would have been to get on the Broadway Extension and go down to I-40, and then west.

It had been several years since I was a big shot Congressman. Only a few blocks away from the Capital Building a tingle ran down my back. I turned by wipers on intermittant as the rain picked up.

"You don't have permission to drive by here" a voice in my head repeated several times.

"Sixteen some odd years ago, I worked here. I could have named my price many times, had anything, and done anything.

Now I am one of the biggest low life's in Oklahoma. Talk about high's and low's this might be in the top ten."

I turned the lights on and the wiper up to full speed, as I turned into my old parking place in the East End parking lot.

"Reserved-Dist. 2" the sign said. I had barely stopped, when the capital police pulled behind the prison pickup.

"Get out of there, this is a reserved area." the Capital Security guy said. Some people know instantly when their life makes a turn. Some may have to wait a while, and still not be able to give you an exact time or place.

As I pulled out of the parking area and headed back to the prison, I am reminded of the exact second by life was put on the rocky road to this hell.

It was the damn water transfer bill that took me down. Had I recognized it at the time what would I have done different?

On April 28, 1978, at 5:02 in the afternoon, I ended the Legislative Session and put my family and myself on a trail that leads from the top of the mountain down too the bottom of the ocean.

When I was a pledge at the University of Oklahoma, I was asked, "how low are you". Too Which I was required to reply, "I am so low that whale shit on the bottom of the ocean looks like white billowy clouds over the gates of hell.

I had told Governor Boren that I would support his Water Bill as long as it was for development and not for Water Transfer to Western Oklahoma.

The bill had been put in my committee and as Chairman I was allowed to do anything I wanted with it. So, I promised everyone in Eastern Oklahoma, "If it has anything to do with transfer it will *never pass.*"

The newspaper in Sallisaw quoted former Mayor Perry Wheeler telling the Mayor of Muldrow, Bill Ed Mabary, and Mayor of Sallisaw, George Glenn: "Parris is going to vote for the Water Transfer Bill. The two mayors replying "how can Parris do this to us I thought he was better than that?" Yes, they had been fooled into thinking Parris was a good guy, but they were wrong.

I had to contend with this front-page crap, month after month, because I had told the owner of the paper, Wheeler Mayo, that I wouldn't meet with his group every Friday morning and do everything they asked.

On April 24, 1978, the Speaker of the House removed the Water Bill from my Committee (this action was legal but never done). I polled the house members and found fifty-six opposed. There were forty-two in favor, and three undecided.

"Take this sentence about water transfer out and I will help you pass it." I told Governor Boren.

"I have to have that language in the bill in order to get the Corps of Engineers to pay for the three million dollar study." He said.

"I just cannot be for this like it is." I said.

"Okay, Fine, you just vote against it and keep your mouth shut. I will allow you to continue on my team, otherwise your dad's State job is history and so is the blacktop from Swan Road to Muldrow, do you understand that? Gov. Boren asked.

"The bill will fail in the House without me saying anything." I advised him.

The Governor showed his teeth and said "I will get it passed, count on it."

I said, "I'm Sorry, David I can't let that happen," and left the governor's office for the last time.

On Friday the 28th day of April 1978, at 8:06 AM, I arrived at work. Five notes from legislators saying they had changed their minds and would vote for the Water Transfer Bill lay of my desk.

I called Senator Herb Rozell and told him the bill was going to pass in the House. He was not surprised.

"The governor is passing out roads, bridges, and jobs, like there is no tomorrow." Senator Rozell said.

"It will sure pass in the senate," he added.

I called Rep. John Monks, "This damm thing is going to pass, sure as shit," I said.

"That fucking little queer is promising his nuts off. He had the damn Highway Commissioner from Muskogee come to my motel room last night and beg me to not speak against the governor's number one program.

Then, this morning the Governor's little pimp, Dusty Martin, was passing out written confirmation on some of Boren's promises.

I still think we have fifty-one solid votes." Rep. Monks said.

"I sure hope so, but I feel the train coming down the track." I replied.

I called Speaker Willis, "Where are you on this water transfer thing?" I asked.

"I'll vote against it, but I promised the Governor I would stay completely out of the House Chamber during the debate, just before the shutoff I will come in and hit the no button and close the count." Speaker Willis said,

Then he added. Bob, David is twisting arms and calling in favors. There is something more to this than we know about now. If he gets after you, I don't think you will be able to win re-election."

I said, "You know I wasn't even going to run again anyway, and my dad is ready to retire. What else can he do?"

"Teachers, lobbyist, state workers, and their relatives, will be against you and you can't win," Speaker Willis said.

I said, "I care, you know that. I have made eight races and won them all, I have never even had a close count. I would like to go out a winner, everybody does."

"You know I have to come back in order to get the payoff for all the hard work I've done the past six years. The north/south turnpike from Kansas to Texas, built through Sequoyah and Adair Counties will be worth millions of dollars to the people, and give me something I can be proud of in my old age."

If he gets me beat, at least, I will have kept the faith the people had in me and made an honest effort.

A man should never make a decision based on coming back or getting re-elected, but they do it all the time.

"The people have much more to lose than I do. I owe my supporters two more years."

"It's your funeral, just be careful this may cost you more than you think." Speaker Bill Willis advised.

At 3:00 PM I went to Senator Rozell. "You got to filibuster this bill, stall for time, think of something."

"Oh, Bob, I can't do that, David would kill me," he said.

Dusty Martin was a real cute young boy from Checotah, Oklahoma. How he became Governor Boren's Legislative liaison was easy for Rep. Monks from Muskogee to figure out. Anyway, a few minutes past four in the afternoon, Dusty sent a note to me, on the house floor. It read: Vote against the bill—keep your mouth shut, and you will remain on the team.

At 4:23 the Water Bill passed the Senate and came to the house for final passage.

Each side is allowed 20 minutes. I told all those on my team, to drain the time as much as possible, but I never told them why.

At 4:45 two more members came by and said they were voting in favor of the Bill.

At 4:47 I begin the final argument in opposition to passage of the Governor's Water Transfer Bill, knowing if a vote were to be taken at that moment, the Governor would win and Water from my District would be shipped to Western Oklahoma.

For years, people in Eastern Oklahoma were denied water from a lake just over the hill. It was just impossible for me to see how a study to ship it 300 miles away would be a good idea.

I told the other members of the House the three-page bill was nothing but a Transfer Bill and it should not be called anything else.

When I finished it was 4:57. Representative Charley Morgan came to the podium as the final speaker in support of the bill.

Had he simply moved do pass on the bill and forget about making a five-minute speech it would have been over and the bill would have passed by at least three votes.

One minute into his time allotment, the clock was covered with a small American Flag in order to keep everyone from knowing when it was 5:00 PM—the time set for sine die adjournment.

At 5:02 my political career and the 36th Legislative Session ended when I removed the flag and exposed the time.

I knew Governor Boren would become Oklahoma's next U.S. Senator, but I would never have imagined him putting me in a Federal Prison.

Would I have done anything different? Maybe, I'm not really all that brave and I would not have wanted my family to go through this hell, if I could have avoided it.

29

The Holdover Unit is an especially cruel part of the Federal Prison System. They ship all prisoners, not holding most favored status (those with money and connections) from all over the Federal Country to this Place in Oklahoma.

After being held long enough to make any other place seem like paradise, they ship you to you're assigned prison.

I was there when a snitch was pitched from the fourth floor cage to the concrete below. He lay there making gurgling sounds for several minutes before he died. They called him "Snitch or Rat."

The Fed's had made him too good of a deal. So, in order to correct their mistake, the snitch was shipped to the Holdover Unit along with the people he snitched out. Bingo, problem solved.

Before 1995, the Holdover Unit was in a 200'x150' building, built like a barn. Only instead of putting hay inside, the Fed's put a four-story cage with stares in the middle. Each floor of the cage was separated into four sections (A, B, C, & D).

My cell was 406D. Which put me on the top floor in the northwest corner. All cells faced the outside. "Snitch" was five doors down in 411D.

We were driven, like cattle, from this big barn to the Cafeteria in the middle of the prison compound at El Reno FCI. After eating, we lined up at the door and were driven back. All the regular El Reno prisoners were separated from us. They would line up on our route from the Holdover building to the cafeteria, or, yell out the windows and throw things to us—like cigarettes, candy, quarters, ECT.

"Lock down, Lock down, go to you house," was always being yelled as you re-entered the barn of a building. We were locked in a small cage all day, except for three trips for meals a day, and going to the Recreation yard four times a week for an hour each time. And, clean up time in the evening.

Odell was my Cellmate. He was from North Hollywood, California. We played chess, discussed our injustice, and slept.

He was in federal custody for transporting Cocaine from LA to Indianapolis, Indiana. He said he hired a girl to carry the drugs and followed along as another passenger. His mule delivered the drugs to Odell's brother-in-law in Indianapolis and went back to California.

Odell hung around visiting with his sister and other friends.

When the DEA raided the home of his brother-in-law, Odell was having a beer in the kitchen. His brother-in-law made a deal and gave him up.

Three years ago, they shipped him from Indiana to Oklahoma for two weeks then back to Terra Haute.

Now, he was coming from Terra Haute, Indiana to Oklahoma on his was to Terminal Island, California, for the reminder of his seven year sentence.

I would not want to be around the brother-in-law when Odell gets out.

From six until nine o'clock in the evening everything in the Holdover Unit is opened up for shake down's and cleaning. All the floors, the entire building is open inside.

The Guards want to make sure you can't escape, but they could care less what the inmates do to other inmates.

Especially if there is a killing being planned for a worthless lowlife.

A lot of important looking people came and took pictures of this "Rat", but nothing was ever done about the three guys who threw him over, in fact, the report said—suicide.

They put chicken wire up outside the rail and that was it.

The Holdover Unit is presently in a new facility on the FAA section of Will Rogers International Airport in Oklahoma City. I read in the newspaper every now and then that a holdover has hanged him self and I wonder. From where I have been I guess I will always question things like this. When a poor person is indicted I always pray he is guilty because he is going to prison, forget about it.

My first Thanksgiving in prison was spent in the Holdover Unit at FCI El Reno. I will never forget it. I went to LaTuna (near El Paso) and arrived back in El Reno for my second Turkey day.

In prison, Thanksgiving is about a little better food for one day. No one in prison is thankful for a damn thing. It would be easy to get mad at someone that showed outward signs of being thankful.

Christmas is different. It's about the birthday of Christ. The only part you have to ignore is the "commercial hype."

30

Bill Ed Brooks sent my Aunt a copy of the CPA Audit the Owner's of the Investment Company had performed in June '86. At the trial, Tom Vest and Bill Ford testified there was no Audit performed on the Company. The CPA Audit was further proof the government fabricated evidence and committed perjury.

I filed a motion for a new trail based on this newly discovered evidence. It was "Brady Material" and should have been given to the Defense. Withholding exculpatory evidence is a reversible error. Perjury is a reversible error.

Craig Bryant said he received the evidence it was not withheld from him.

Tom Vest presented a signed affidavit stating he handed a copy of the CPA Audit over to Craig Bryant.

The honorable Judge Seay stated in his Order denying the motion, that as manager of the Company it would be ignorant for anyone to believe Parris would not know of the Audit. Hello Judge Seay, I was gone from the Company on May 16th. The Owners had the Audit performed in June. Now, how the hell would I know about something done after I was gone?

They told the Court an Audit of the Company was never performed. It might be said that you, Judge Seay, should have known about this audit during the trial and protected me from these crooks. You would save yourself all these rulings you have to make to protect them.

Okay, If Craig Bryant was handed this Exculpatory CPA Audit and failed to use it to gain a not guilty verdict from the jury, its malpractice. So, I filed a Compliant against Craig Bryant for Legal Malpractice.

The prosecutor and agent advise the Court that they gave no evidence to Craig Bryant. He had no chance to use the Audit for the Defense, because he did not have it.

Now, lets see he had it, and he did not have it. What is important to remember is that we are in America and the court system is always fair.

The CPA Audit proves the Portfolio Manager invested all the money and never diverted any to his personal use, and therefore, not guilty. That is the important thing.

If you were found guilty of killing John Brown and your lawyer failed to call John Brown as a witness in your favor. Later, you filed a motion for a new trial and advised the Court you intend to present John Brown at the hearing. The court denied your motion. You filed an appeal with the appeals court and included an affidavit from John Brown indicating he was alive during the trial.

The appeals court denied your motion. They find the pleading to be a copulation and not understandable.

You might get a little freaked out, like me.

31

In March '96, I went to the Halfway house in Oklahoma City. Finding work is another handicap a convicted felon in burdened with. In addition to the Court sentence, there is the life sentence being a convicted felon brings.

The number of jobs a felon may apply for, and his parole officer will allow him to accept are limited.

The bitter truth is that seven out of ten inmates on parole will return to prison within a short period of time mostly for minor, non-jail time offenses. Any violation of the law gets you back inside. Not buckling your seat belt, getting a Speeding ticket, unpaid debts, parking tickets, visiting a friend whom has a gun in the bedroom.

A parolee loses a job and can't find another one within ten days, he's back inside. Charge something and let the bill get past due, and your back inside. Have a medical problem and your back inside.

In the new version of us, we are going to make it easier to find employment ($7.00 per hour is much less than $25,000 a year). And, violating parole must involve a crime that would ordinarily require jail time.

Not $55.00 dollar fines kind of offense. I was lucky Louis McAlpine helped me get a job with a law firm in Oklahoma City, but I could see how much being a convicted felon affected the other guys. I was just lucky to have friends like Wayne and Louie.

All of those in the half-way-house were making a world class effort and you wanted so badly to be able to help the ones that just couldn't seem to get it done. Some see they are going back to prison and run. This is what the Government wants. Now they got you for three more years. Cost the taxpayers another $75,000 bucks.

Other problems followed a felon. I purchased a Car from Hudiburg Buick in Oklahoma City, at the "guaranteed lowest price" of $25,611. Two days later, HUDIBURG advertised the same car for $21,545. I called about this lowest price guarantee. They offered me an extra oil change. I called Vance Motors and found out they had the same equipment on a blue Buick LaSabre they had been trying to sale for the past month at $20,889.

I filed Court Action against HUDIBURG. But because I was a convicted felon HUDIBURG knew they could screw me and their lawyer got Judge Ricks to order me into binding arbitration with another lawyer making the ruling.

I told the arbitrator I had not signed any agreement with Hudiburg to settle this was. I showed him the card from Hudiburg that had "Lowest price guaranteed" written on it. Not the lowest prices in town or always the low price. Nothing like that. This was like Circuit City, you got 30 days to shop and Hudiburg writes you a check if you find a lower price.

Hudiburg got a $5,000 judgment against me.

Another case of felon bashing was when I was run over by a little old lady on West Reno and MacArthur. Allstate Insurance fixed by car before they found out I was a felon.

They refused to pay my medical bills and I filed court action. Allstate was very smart in their refusal to help me and my lawyer said I should settle for anything they offered. "After all you have to remember you are a felon and a jury will not look with favor on you." My lawyer said.

For a year I refused to accept any offer. I just wanted to take it to court and see if a jury was really like that.

When we took depositions a month before the jury trial was scheduled, Allstate found out the lady who ran the red light was also a convicted felon, she had killed her first husband and served seven years for it. Allstate paid my claim in full.

32

I contacted Oklahoma University President, David Lyle Boren, and asked him to call his Judge off and help get me a fair trial. I'm sure he got a good laugh out of that.

He knew Judge Seay was the biggest alcoholic in Law School. Just because he was Seminole, Oklahoma——Is that why Boren appointed him to such an important, Permanent job? Here lies David L. Boren, he appointed A drunk to rule Eastern Oklahoma for thirty years. Is that what we will put on his tomb stone?

(You would be correct to note, at this point, that the author is quite honestly put out by the lack of justice he received at the Hands of the Honorable Judge; however several people who were law students at the same time as Frank Seay reported this fact to me).

Boren's appointee, Judge Frank Howell Seay, gave me 15 years on a guideline sentence of none to 15 months.

The Judge said, "Your lawyer did a fine job." He gave no other reason for handing down the New World record sentence for a first time offender involving anything less than murder.

Banks and Investment Company's report the amount on deposit, and the amount of loans outstanding. On a bank or Investment Company monthly statement are the amounts on deposit.

They are required to account for this money (not all the money you put into the account over the years—Just the amount on deposit at a given time).

In my case, the Government was allowed to add not only each month to a yearly total, but a six-year running total. The $1.8 Million invested, represented money that was invested—withdrawn and re-invested several times.

Banks and Merrill Lynch reduce the amount withdrawn from the deposits to show the total amount on deposit. They could show the total amount a customer deposited over a twenty year period at say seventy million dollars, but they would only be liable for the amount on deposit at the time of the inquire, Not the entire seventy million dollars.

The only thing a stockbroker adds is the income or loss. At no time during the five-year period was I managing more than $650,000.

The amount needed to look bigger, so Agent Vest used some "fuzzy" math to the case look bigger and grab more press, I guess.

Eleven Investors and I were in the Company. They put money in and took money out. I put money in and took money out. There was never other people putting money in so I could return the first investor's money to him or her or me. I never removed more money that I had in the Company. I never removed my mother's money or that of my wife, Carol's, when I left the Company.

I could have easily done that, and now I see that I should have.

Special FBI Agent, Tom Vest, knew he was telling a lie to the Jury when he made the statement "This was a Ponzi Scheme." This false statement to the jury must have inflamed the Jury because it sure shocked me. The newspapers made a big deal out of it.

I found that in nine hundred cases involving Investments and the Defendant stuck with a Federal Defense Attorney, the FBI claimed they were "classic Ponzi Schemes." Ponzi took the first investor's money for himself, then used the second investor funds to return money to the first one.

A real Attorney would have set Vest's hair on fire for his lies and the U.S. Attorney would have not liked the outcome quite so much. A poor person with a Federal Defense Attorney appointed for him allows the court and everybody to get through a case much more quickly.

"We save time, energy, and money." John Raley said. "We know they're guilty before we file for an indictment." He added.

If all the people indicted by a U.S. Attorney in the United States were to have a fair trial it would backup the system so badly that several thousand criminals would go free just because of the time constraints.

Have you ever noticed a trial for a rich person takes two months or more and he usually wins. A poor person has a two-day trial and goes to jail.

What can be done? Hire investigators in the Public Defenders Office. Make sure they are as good as the FBI Agents, even at lying. Have a laboratory for testing FBI, DEA,

State, County, and City Law Enforcement Agencies chemical Results to make sure they are correct.

When the FBI says it's a Classic Ponzi Scheme or a Perfect Bundy Murder, there will be Special Agent from the Public Defender's Office ready to explain to the Jury that this conclusion cannot be correct, unless it is. In which case the man will pled guilty.

Another necessary thing is for the Public Defender to have two or three Lawyers assist during the trial. It looks bad for an innocent person to only have one lawyer. When, like in my case, John Raley had three lawyers and the Special Agent is setting next to the Jury.

I know the Jury overheard them talking about the overwhelming case against me. I could see them nod their heads every time another one of them was making a point.

Lastly, require all Federal Judges to personally interview the person soon after he is found guilty.

Ask questions like: (a) What do you have that was not presented at the trial? (b) Any witnesses not called? (c) Any question of a witness you wanted asked that wasn't asked? (d) Let me look at any Documents you believe should have been used at your trail. (e) What about government documents? Can you prove any errors were made on them?

A twenty-minute interview might keep an innocent person from going to prison, and would cut down on the number of appeals and re-consideration motions filling up the Court System.

I met several other people Mr. Bryant's brilliant defense put in prison. I figure he alone cost the taxpayers over four million dollars from 1990 through 1998. And he made twenty-one innocent families suffer.

The fastest growing business in America is our Prison System. That is not a good thing to say for the land of the free.

Too many laws making anything we do illegal are only part of the problem. The greatest advance in the percentage of people going to prison is plea-bargaining. We have allowed this to happen because we cannot find a better solution. Prosecutors offer a deal in exchange for a plea of guilty. You say no. They say:

"Okay, we are going to charge your mother."

"My mother had nothing do with drug dealing."

"We got a guy who will say she delivered two grams to him only last week."

"My God man, you can't go after my mother, she's seventy-six years old, for Christ sake."

"Pled guilty, get three years, or, we take your mother's old wrinkled ass to jail."

Think this only happens in the movies? Think again, this goes on all the time. I was in prison with several that wanted a trial for themselves, but gave up when their mother, father, brother, sister, ECT, were going to be charged.

Plea-bargaining can't be done away with, and if the mother delivered drugs she should be charged. It should never be part of another person's plea agreement.

Beating on me is okay, but I don't want you beating on my mother, or my wife and children. The time involved should not be more than two or three year's less.

The Death Penalty should be done away with unless it involves mass murder or the killing of law enforcement people when they are doing their duty to protect and defend.

You can look at the killing of a baby by its daddy and want him included. The way our system is today innocent people are going to prison if they are poor. The appeals system isn't much help when looking at the big picture. Mexicans and Blacks are arrested seventeen times more often than Asian's and Caucasian's. Why is that?

I saw a twenty-five years old Mexican man receive a 30 years sentence. His trial lasted Eighteen minutes. The Special Agent who was to testify about the drug bust was in prison in Tennessee for withholding and selling cocaine (he is really special).

Judge Frank Howell Seay said "this the last time I am going to sentence one of these Mexicans without you having the arresting officer at the trial."

Yes, he pled not guilty to cocaine sales. No one could testify the Mexican was guilty. The public defender told the judge his client harvested his Marihuana crop and brought it to America to sell, but he never had anything to do with any cocaine.

A female DEA agent was the only witness. She said she heard the arresting office (who is now in prison) say, over the radio, "he has cocaine." That's it.

John Raley said, "Your Honor this man is guilty of both and should be punished for both."

Well, he sure was—Thirty years. That is a very long time. Try 30 days sometime and you will agree Three years should be the maximum sentence for a first time non-violent, offense.

Poor people and Mexicans should not be used to keep private prisons in business. And, when we start cutting the fat out of overspending, the first place to look would be the amount of money we are spending on the losing war on drugs.

Keep them out of the Country, if we can, but stop putting junkies in prison. We have millions of greedy people in America. There is no doubt in my mind the FBI could arrest an additional million people next month. They could walk up to a stranger in any town and offer him $5,000 to deliver a package to North Fifth and Main Street. Fifteen out of twenty would do it.

Why are so many Drug Lab's popping up all over the Country? Think about two hundred thousand junkies going to jail each year. These people meet five thousand junkies who have been inside for several years. Everyone finds out how to make that shit and they pass the information to the next generation of dope heads.

Work is hard for a felon to find and making "speed" is the easiest thing in the world. I learned how to make it the first two weeks into my sentence and I didn't even want to know.

How to grow and cultivate marijuana. Where all the connections are for International opium, cocaine, and heroin. I am now better trained to be a criminal than an accountant and the pay is much better.

I can't get an accounting license because I am a felon. See how things push in the wrong direction? We need to change all that in non-violent cases. I could go to Brownsville, Texas, purchase drugs for $10,000 bring them back to Oklahoma City and sell them for $20,000.

A former Mexican cellmate told me he made $25,000 for each trip to Chicago. If he can just make three or four trips before getting caught, it's worth it. Where else could he make $75,000, so quick? And, when he is caught he spends three years in prison costing the taxpayers while his brother delivers the next three loads of illegal drugs.

33

Ten years has passed since my illegal conviction. Sixteen appeals have been denied without even a hearing for the Honorable Court to know the facts. My Constitutional Rights to Life, Liberty, and Freedom was denied without so much as a second glance by any higher Court.

Do you have any of your family in prison? Well, get ready because you will. When they wanted to build several building with Revenue Sharing money in 1974, I said they would not qualify as a "one time" expense (at the time, none of the members of the House or Senate wanted to spend revenue sharing on something that would cost more every year).

When the State bought all that property in 1978, to build parking lots around the State Capital, I said they would be overflowing in less than two years. Of course, I was correct. It's like that *Field of Dreams* movie.

Today, I am telling you if we built a million prisons, our Government will fill them up.

At the rate we are putting people in prison I predict there will be Fifteen Million People incarcerated in 2020. Two million will be innocent. Four Million will be women. And, when they hit the street again, you will not be thanked.

People on death row are being found not guilty because of DNA testing. No one has asked how 12 men and women could possibly have found him guilty in the first place. There are far more innocent people in regular prison than there are on Death Row.

There is no miracle relief for the two thousand innocent people serving three to fifteen years, like DNA is doing for the innocent on Death Row.

How about forming a review committee made up of non-lawyer (real people) with a little common sense. Put someone on the committee who can see whether a person is suffering the kind of pain only an innocent person knows about.

Wouldn't it be great if a thousand of the two thousand poor innocent inmates, in Federal Prison, could go home? At twenty-five thousand dollars per head, per year, think how much money our Government could save.

When I figure out how we get the guilty rich in jail, where they belong, I will write another book. Until that time, my advice is for you to get rich and become part of the privileged class of people in the United States of America. If you have a deep desire to steal from your neighbor make sure your first money goes into a Legal System Funding Account. With $50,000 the odds are much better that you will walk.

Epilogue

The water seemed a little darker for this time of year. A little more decay was causing dark particles to rise up from the bottom.

For most folks it's just another dog day in early August. For Annie Mae it seemed this was the day she had been waiting for her entire life.

The little four-man boat moved along side the wooden boat dock across the Arkansas State Highway from Lake Village.

The woman and her two young girls got out and took their basket of food and drinks up to picnic tables next to the highway.

"Gonna be another warm one" the mother said, as much to the small cloud overhead as too either of the children.

The youngest girl had wanted a pop from almost the first moment she set foot in the boat. The mother opened a can of Coke and handed it to the pretty four-year-old girl.

"You want one, shawna?"

The trip across the water from home only took twenty minutes, but without a motor, and only one paddle, which Shawna insisted on using, eleven year old Shawna was plumb dune in and plopped down on the dry grass and worked at catching her breath.

"In a minute". She replied.

"Tell me again why we had to meet Grandpa over here?"

"How would you expect him to find our place?"

"How come he never been to see us before?"

"I done told you a thousand times, he's been out of the Country?"

"What kind of work would keep him away this long?

"That would be a good question for you to ask him, when he gets here, now wouldn't it."

Shalicia took a few sips from the can of pop and begin beating a tree with a stick she picked up on the ground.

"Mama, is Grandpa gonna like me?" Shalicia asked.

"Ain't no doubt about it. It will be love at first sight for both you girls. And, you gonna love him too."

"Well, when is he gonna get here, then?"

"He said ten and its only 9:30, we is early?"

"I want to show Grandpa my doll, why didn't you let me bring my doll?"

"We gonna take him back in the boat after we have lunch, if he'll go with us. You can show him your doll then, can't you?"

"Mama, I got to go!" Shawna said

"Okay, take your sisters hand and we will all go across the highway to the service station."

When the old man pulled up in his old Ford Pickup he could see the picnic basket on the table, but no one was around.

He got out of his truck and put presents on an empty picnic table. He looked across the highway for anybody. He was a little early.

That basket on the other table could belong to anyone.

He brought Annie Mae a gold wristwatch. Shawna a basketball and an orange and white plastic basketball hoop with an adjustable pole. For Shalicia he had purchased a windup toy that walked around beating on a drum.

He also brought five pounds of BBQ Beef, a jar of dill pickles, some buns, a big bag of potato chips, and two six pack's of Pepsi.

He looked back towards Lake Village as two beautiful little girls racing towards him with their arms in the air. He takes two or three steps in their direction before dropping to his knees. When the little girls arrived and jumped into his big old arms, he lifted them up high in the air as he kissed them twice on each side of their faces.

He set the children down and begins crying as the daughter he hadn't seen in twenty-seven years slowly approached him.

"I'm so sorry for all the pain I've caused you." He said.

"Daddy! Daddy! I am so happy to see you again. I just really can't believe you're here. I never though I would look in your eyes and get to hug your neck again.

They held each other for a long while before setting down and eating.

It seemed to set in silence and enjoy reading each others faces overcome all the questions and other talking stuff for the moment.

After a while the little group loaded the boat and pushed off for home.

It was Wednesday afternoon, around 4 p.m., when my phone rang.

"Hello" I said.

"Hello, is this Mr. Parris?" The man asked.

"Yes, it is, who is this?" I replied.

"Did you used to be the Town Driver at El Reno?" MJ Asked.

"YOU SON OF A GUN…you found your daughter.

About the Author

Bob O. Parris lives in Oklahoma City, with his wife, Carol, and three Westie's. He is currently writing another True Story *"MOON SHADOWS."*

Mr. Parris served in the Oklahoma Legislature from 1972-78 and was on the Sallisaw City Counsel for four years 1968-72. He served in the U.S. Navy, and is a Former Member of the Jaycees, Rotary and Masonic Lodge.

Mr. Parris attended The University of Oklahoma and Tulsa University.

He was a Public Accountant for 25 years.

Appendix

1. Audit Report (3 pages).
2. Letter to Judge Seay.
3. Fabricated Government Document.
4. Original FBI Document (3 pages).
5. Copy of Insurance Policy (2 pages).
6. Copy of Bank Loans.
7. Testimony denying a CPA Audit was performed.
8. Copy of the $32,000 Check.
9. Copy of the Investment Company's Check.
10. Typical government remark.
11. Mr. Ford said "some" money withdrawn. (Some = $331,000.
12 The AUDITED amount lost by Individuals.
13. Motion for New Attorney, before Illegal Trial started.

Audit Statement (continued)

The following reports are made using Bank Statements, Brokerage Firm's, records, and owner investment Receipt and Disbursement Reports. Also, FBI Agent Tom Vest's statements, and those of the CPA Audit prepared on June 27, 1986. The accounts presented are made In accordance with Generally Accepted Accounting Principles. The Opinions expressed are using Generally Accepted Auditing Standards. The only bank account for the Parris Management Trust was found in Fayetteville Arkansas. The account activity for the period in Question:

August 1, 1984. Beginning Balance	$582,167.08
Investment 8-1-84 to 1-1-85	8,300.00
Withdrawals 8-1-84 to 1-1-85	(35,610.00)
Gain (Loss) on investments	(40,993.66)
January 1, 1985. Ending Balance	$545,962.75

FBI Agent Tom Vest testified in Federal Court at Muskogee, Oklahoma: (1.) Money from this fund was used to purchase a $200,000 dollar Chevy Dealership. (2.) Money from this fund was used to purchase a $100,000 dollar Dog, and (3.) A $100,000 dollars was paid from this fund to purchase an Airplane.

As anyone can see, the investment fund had Very light activity during the period. The amounts received, deposited, and withdrawn, would suggest the money to purchase anything more that $43,000 dollars would be *completely impossible (i.e. if all the receipts and withdrawals were diverted to Other interests there are only $43,000 available).*

We now turn are attention to Parris Management Service Inc. in Sallisaw, Oklahoma. Bob O. Parris and his family incorporated this checking account in 1979. We Audited the

Checking Account for the same period as the Trust's (above), and found:

Balance (8-1-84)	$30,129.18

Receipts:	
Breeding Fees	$ 64,500.00
Airplane Receipts	8,742.10
Loan from Commercial Bank	$ 250,000.00
Trust Investors	8,300.00
Tampa Greyhound Track	81,217.00
West Palm Beach Track	46,813.09
Sale of Accounting Business	85,000.00
Local Investment Inc.	30,000.00
Midnight Blue Inc.	23,112.00
Total Receipts	$597,684.19

Disbursements:	
Purchase Airplane	$ 18,500.00
Purchase Dog	100,000.00
Purchase Chevy Dealership	201,183.29
Greyhound Expense	85,081.76
Local Investment Inc.	15,000.00
Investment Deposit	8,300.00
Improvements Sallisaw Farm	119,266.05
Total Disbursements	$(547,331.10)
Balance (1-1-85)	$80,482.27

We reviewed the Bank Loan proceeds and the timing of the payments to the Chevy Dealership Construction Company. The Dog Income - bank loan and payments for the Dog. And, the Airplane purchase of $18,500. FBI Agent Tom Vest was Mistaken in his testimony beginning on Page 265 and continuing through 280. We found FBI Agent, Tom Vest's, testimony to be—*without question, untrue. (Agent Vest is defeated by his own accounting reports)*

To complete the, investments, withdrawals, and balances, examination for the Investment Trust—We present two final Receipt and Disbursement Schedules.

Balance (1-1-85)	$545,962.75
Investments	170,125.00
Withdrawals	(210,125.00)
Gain (Loss) for the period.	(43,469.77)
Balance (1-1-86)	$308,949.27
From 1-1-86 to 5-16-86	
Balance (1-1-86)	$308,949.27
Investments	32,000.00
Withdrawals	(46,119.81)
Gain (Loss) on	
investments for the period.	36,217.74

Balance in the Account when Bob O. Parris left the company, and the amount Bill Ford became responsible for it on May 17, 1986: $331,047.20 Mr. Ford kept all this money. See, on page 57 of the Trial Transcript he said he removed "some"—then on page 58 he said "There was a little bit." When pressed on page 58 Mr. Ford said "$90,000. Then, on page 59, he admitted there was actually two withdrawals the second one "was "one hundred 25 thousand." The Audit report shows Mr. Ford received $331,047.20. He could have lost additional investor funds in the Stock Market after May 17, 1986.

Mr. Ford admits (after saying he took out "some" and "a little bit") to taking out $215,000.00 for his personal use. The audit figures seem to indicate he removed well over $300,000, and likely the $331,000 amount claimed by Mr. Parris.

Mr. Bill Ford was the Trustee in charge of the Accounting for the Investment Trust. When asked if an Audit was ever made, Mr. Ford said NO. We found the Audit Report prepared by the CPA Firm in Ft. Smith, Arkansas. Mr. Ford had this Audit done after Mr. Parris was gone from the Investment Trust leaving Mr. Ford in charge of managing the assets of the Company as well as getting the Audit done.

His denial that an audit was ever performed is on page 60 of the Trial Transcript.

May 15, 2001

Frank H. Seay, Judge
U.S. District Court
Federal Courthouse
Muskogee, OK 74401
RE: CR-019-91-S

Dear Judge Seay:

My motion for a new trial is attached. I hope you will allow me, at least, a hearing. Clearly, the Government lied about everything material to the case and I should get a new trial.

Before my trial, I asked you to appoint me a new Attorney. I advised you Mr. BRYANT was not going to subpoena any of my witnesses. He had not even looked at my documented evidence. He stipulated to several thousand sheets of paper and two depositions I have never seen, against my orders.

At the trial, none of my witnesses or documents was presented to show the Court and Jury, I was telling the truth and the government Lied. BRYANT conspired with RALEY, VEST, and others. They also, aid and abetted and obstructed justice in and outside the Courtroom.

After the trial, I filed a motion for a new trial. Listed more than ninety errors made by Mr. BRYANT. That motion was denied early the next morning, without a hearing.

Later, my family found a copy of the CPA Audit made of the company (after I was gone). This Audit completely supported my Accounting Reports and Testimony. It stands today as only one of ninety documents that *Clearly* proves BRYANT, RALEY, VEST, and others committed perjury, aided and abetted, conspired, and other criminal activities, at my trial.

I am Innocent, only Government Lies proved otherwise. Nothing you can do will bring back what VEST, BRYANT, RALEY, AND OTHERS have stolen. However; Ten years of injustice can begin to end, today, with a fair trial.

Respectfully,

BOB O. PARRIS

SUMMARY OF VICTIMS INVESTMENTS WITH PARRIS FROM
1980 1987

MONEY FROM VICTIMS TO PARRIS	2,010,735.22
SECURITIES FROM VICTIMS TO PARRIS	498,942.46
TOTAL VICTIMS INVESTED WITH PARRIS:	$2,509,677.68
LESS INVESTORS DEDUCTIONS:	
MONEY PARRIS RETURNED TO VICTIMS	(592,583.47)
SECURITIES RETURNED TO VICTIMS	(420,330.07)
LOSSES FROM INVESTMENTS	(605,911.49)

TOTAL INVESTORS DEDUCTIONS	$(1,618,725.03)

VICTIMS MONEY TO BE	
ACCOUNTED FOR:	890,952.65
AMOUNT PARRIS SPENT	
FOR PERSONAL USE	(889,008.85

AMOUNT REMAINING IN ACCOUNT	$1,943.80
	=============

GOVERNMENT
EXHIBIT 99

ALL INVESTORS TRANSACTION DETAIL

1. DATE CLEARED	2. INVESTOR	3. DEPOSITS	4. WITHDRAWS	5. SOURCE/ ACCOUNT	6. SOURCE/ CHECK#	7. DEPOSIT/ ACCOUNT	8. DEP OTH/ PERS ACCT	9. CUM +DEP	10. CUM -WTD	11. R/B
1/14/80	JM	13,250.00				FNB-030		13,250.00	0.00	13,250.00
5/1/80	BF	28,000.00		NBS-206	638	FNB-030		41,250.00	0.00	41,250.00
5/5/80	JM	62,000.00		ML-063		FNB-030		103,250.00	0.00	103,250.00
5/16/80	JM	40,000.00		FNB-938	153	AGE-530		143,250.00	0.00	143,250.00
5/27/80	JM	7,000.00		FNB-938	155	AGE-530		150,250.00	0.00	150,250.00
6/4/80	JM	10,000.00		FNB-938	163	AGE-530		160,250.00	0.00	160,250.00
6/4/80	JM	1,850.60		AGE-530		AGE-530		162,100.60	0.00	162,100.60
7/1/80	JM		620.00	FNB-030	343			162,100.60	620.00	161,480.60
7/25/80	BF	10,000.00		NBS-206	761	FNB-030		172,100.60	620.00	171,480.60
7/28/80	JM		3,863.57	AGE-530				172,100.60	4,483.57	167,617.03
7/29/80	JM		3,663.51	AGE-530				172,100.60	8,147.08	163,953.52
7/30/80	JM		1,490.55	AGE-530				172,100.60	9,637.63	162,462.97
7/31/80	JM		508.72	AGE-530				172,100.60	10,146.35	161,954.25
8/15/80	BF	10,000.00		NBS-101	5089	FNB-030		182,100.60	10,146.35	171,954.25
8/21/80	JM	18,000.00		FNB-938	178	FNB-030		200,100.60	10,146.35	189,954.25
8/29/80	JM		1,850.60	AGE-530				200,100.60	11,996.95	188,103.65
9/3/80	JM		3,000.00	AGE-530				200,100.60	14,996.95	185,103.65
9/8/80	JJ	2,564.77				FNB-030		202,665.37	14,996.95	187,668.42
9/10/80	JM		163.00	AGE-530				202,665.37	15,159.95	187,505.42
9/11/80	JJ	12,435.23		AGE-662	1	FNB-030		215,100.60	15,159.95	199,940.65
9/24/80	BF	10,926.00				FNB-030		226,026.60	15,159.95	210,866.65
9/26/80	JM	10,000.00				FNB-030		236,026.60	15,159.95	220,866.65
10/1/80	JJ	16,190.59				FNB-030		252,217.19	15,159.95	237,057.24
10/6/80	JM		208.69	AGE-530				252,217.19	15,368.64	236,848.55
11/11/80	JM		226.82	AGE-530				252,217.19	15,595.46	236,621.73
12/16/80	JM		485.58	AGE-530				252,217.19	16,081.04	236,136.15
1/7/81	JM	5,000.00		FNB-938	193	FNB-030		257,217.19	16,081.04	241,136.15
1/8/81	JJ	20,000.00		FNB-742	4775	FNB-030		277,217.19	16,081.04	261,136.15
1/9/81	JM		348.30	AGE-530				277,217.19	16,429.34	260,787.85
2/12/81	JM		150.90	AGE-530				277,217.19	16,580.24	260,636.95
2/24/81	HL	40,000.00		NBS-106	2804	PHX-396		317,217.19	16,580.24	300,636.95
3/24/81	JM		194.12	AGE-530				317,217.19	16,774.36	300,442.83
3/26/81	JF	504.03		NBS-906	1823	PHX-396		317,721.22	16,774.36	300,946.86
3/26/81	JF	500.00		NBS-801	2496	PHX-396		318,221.22	16,774.36	301,446.86
3/26/81	JF	50,000.00		NBS-906	1825	PHX-396		368,221.22	16,774.36	351,446.86
4/22/81	JM	5,000.00		FNB-938	212	AGE-530		373,221.22	16,774.36	356,446.86
4/22/81	JM		225.12	AGE-530				373,221.22	16,999.48	356,221.74
4/30/81	RS	30,000.00		ABT-460	73713	PHX-396		403,221.22	16,999.48	386,221.74
5/11/81	JM	5,000.00		FNB-938	213	AGE-530		408,221.22	16,999.48	391,221.74
5/20/81	JM		263.72	AGE-530				408,221.22	17,263.20	390,958.02
6/5/81	JF		5,000.00	AGE-417				408,221.22	22,263.20	385,958.02
6/17/81	JJ	12,438.01		AGE-662	3	PHX-396		420,659.23	22,263.20	398,396.03
6/18/81	JM		368.25	AGE-530				420,659.23	22,631.45	398,027.78
7/13/81	JW	10,000.00		NBS7		PHX-396		430,659.23	22,631.45	408,027.78
7/13/81	JW	10,000.00		NBS7		PHX-396		440,659.23	22,631.45	418,027.78
7/16/81	JM		620.00	PHX-396	307			440,659.23	23,251.45	417,407.78
7/24/81	JM	10,000.00		FNB-938	219	PHX-396		450,659.23	23,251.45	427,407.78
7/24/81	JM	90,000.00		FNB-938	221	PHX-396		540,659.23	23,251.45	517,407.78

Page 1

Appendix II
Page 1 of 3

ALL INVESTORS TRANSACTION DETAIL

Date	Inv							
8/7/81	JM		800.00 PHX-396	348		540,659.23	24,051.45	516,607.78
8/21/81	JF		5,000.00 PHX-396	384		540,659.23	29,051.45	511,607.78
8/24/81	JM		620.00 PHX-396	349		540,659.23	29,671.45	510,987.78
9/8/81	JM		13.09 AGE-530			540,659.23	29,684.54	510,974.69
9/10/81	JM		620.00 PHX-396	405		540,659.23	30,304.54	510,354.69
9/16/81	JM	10,000.00	FNB-938	228 AGE-530		550,659.23	30,304.54	520,354.69
9/21/81	JM		14.23 AGE-530			550,659.23	30,318.77	520,340.46
10/9/81	JM		800.00 PHX-396	466		550,659.23	31,118.77	519,540.46
10/23/81	JM		122.89 AGE-530			550,659.23	31,241.66	519,417.57
11/2/81	JW	20,000.00	NBS		PHX-396	570,659.23	31,241.66	539,417.57
11/10/81	JM		800.00 PHX-396	551		570,659.23	32,041.66	538,617.57
11/18/81	JM		137.02 AGE-530			570,659.23	32,178.68	538,480.55
11/20/81	JM	10,000.00	FNB-938	236 AGE-530		580,659.23	32,178.68	548,480.55
12/16/81	JM		800.00 PHX-396 ?			580,659.23	32,978.68	547,680.55
12/21/81	JM		294.62 AGE-530			580,659.23	33,273.30	547,385.93
1/6/82	DR	5,000.00	BOM-673	973 PHX-396		585,659.23	33,273.30	552,385.93
1/6/82	DR	5,000.00	VSB-641	762 PHX-396		590,659.23	33,273.30	557,385.93
1/7/82	JW	15,000.00	NBS-106	292 PHX-396		605,659.23	33,273.30	572,385.93
1/7/82	JW	5,000.00	VSB-923	110 PHX-396		610,659.23	33,273.30	577,385.93
1/20/82	JM		216.06 AGE-530			610,659.23	33,489.36	577,169.87
1/29/82	JM	20,000.00		AGE-530		630,659.23	33,489.36	597,169.87
2/5/82	JJ	15,000.00	FNB-742	5210 PHX-396		645,659.23	33,489.36	612,169.87
2/8/82	JM	10,000.00	FNB-938	252 AGE-530		655,659.23	33,489.36	622,169.87
2/26/82	JM		308.58 AGE-530			655,659.23	33,797.94	621,861.29
3/24/82	JM		438.71 AGE-530			655,659.23	34,236.65	621,422.58
3/26/82	JF	11,700.00	NBS-965	101844 PHX-396		667,359.23	34,236.65	633,122.58
3/26/82	JF	1,500.00	NBS-801	3097 PHX-396		668,859.23	34,236.65	634,622.58
4/1/82	JF	10,076.23	NBS-965	102040 PHX-396		678,935.46	34,236.65	644,698.81
4/7/82	JM		1,000.00 PHX-396	882		678,935.46	35,236.65	643,698.81
4/9/82	JT	1,050.00	NBS-301	571 PHX-396		679,985.46	35,236.65	644,748.81
4/12/82	MC	1,700.00	NBS-306	573 PHX-396		681,685.46	35,236.65	646,448.81
4/26/82	JM		440.64 AGE-530			681,685.46	35,877.29	646,008.17
5/7/82	JF	12,700.00	NBS-965	103568 PHX-396		694,385.46	35,877.29	658,708.17
5/10/82	JM		1,000.00 PHX-396	910		694,385.46	36,677.29	657,708.17
5/12/82	JM		1,000.00 PHX-396	928		694,385.46	37,677.29	656,708.17
5/27/82	JM		303.28 AGE-530			694,385.46	37,980.57	656,404.89
6/15/82	JM		1,000.00 PHX-396	1020		694,385.46	38,980.57	655,404.89
6/16/82	JM		1,000.00 PHX-396	1023		694,385.46	39,980.57	654,404.89
6/24/82	JM		9.18 AGE-530			694,385.46	39,989.75	654,395.71
7/6/82	JM		1,000.00 PHX-396	1062		694,385.46	40,989.75	653,395.71
7/8/82	JM	10,000.00	PHX-347	132 PHX-396		704,385.46	40,989.75	663,395.71
7/15/82	JM		1,000.00 PHX-396	1086		704,385.46	41,989.75	662,395.71
7/21/82	JM		8.59 AGE-530			704,385.46	41,998.34	662,387.12
7/21/82	RS		4,000.00 PHX-396	1088		704,385.46	45,998.34	658,387.12
7/22/82	JM	10,000.00	PHX-347	138 PHX-396		714,385.46	45,998.34	668,387.12
7/22/82	JJ	20,000.00	NBS-965	105070 PHX-396		734,385.46	45,998.34	688,387.12
7/23/82	JF	12,298.28	NBS-965	106108 PHX-396		746,683.74	45,998.34	700,685.40
7/26/82	JM		1,000.00 PHX-396	1110		746,683.74	46,998.34	699,685.40
8/6/82	JM		900.00 PHX-396	1144		746,683.74	47,898.34	698,785.40
8/6/82	JM		1,000.00 PHX-396	1142		746,683.74	48,898.34	697,785.40
8/27/82	JM		9.98 AGE-530			746,683.74	48,908.32	697,775.42
8/30/82	JF	13,400.00	NBS-965	107279 PHX-396		760,083.74	48,908.32	711,175.42
10/5/82	JM		900.00 PHX-396	1106		760,083.74	49,808.32	710,275.42

Page 2

Appendix II
Page 2 of 3

ALL INVESTORS TRANSACTION DETAIL

12/2/85	JM		5,100.00	PHX-396	2401	1,988,735.22	401,769.18 1,586,966.04
12/3/85	JM		2,434.96	PHX-396	2400	1,988,735.22	404,204.14 1,584,531.08
12/4/85	JF		675.00	PHX-396	2398	1,988,735.22	404,879.14 1,583,856.08
12/19/85	JW		600.00	PHX-396	2405	1,988,735.22	405,479.14 1,583,256.08
1/2/86	JM		5,100.00	PHX-396	2410	1,988,735.22	410,579.14 1,578,156.08
1/6/86	JM		2,412.76	PHX-396	2409	1,988,735.22	412,991.90 1,575,743.32
1/22/86	JW		800.00	PHX-396	2423	1,988,735.22	413,791.90 1,574,943.32
2/4/86	JF		675.00	PHX-396	2424	1,988,735.22	414,466.90 1,574,268.32
2/5/86	JM		5,100.00	ML-096	105	1,988,735.22	419,566.90 1,569,168.32
2/5/86	JM		2,309.48	ML-096	104	1,988,735.22	421,876.38 1,566,858.84
2/20/86	JW		800.00	PHX-396	2435	1,988,735.22	422,676.38 1,566,058.84
3/3/86	JM		5,100.00	ML-096	109	1,988,735.22	427,776.38 1,560,958.84
3/3/86	JM		2,618.16	ML-096	108	1,988,735.22	430,394.54 1,558,340.68
3/14/86	JM		2,500.00	ML-096	111	1,988,735.22	432,894.54 1,555,840.68
3/17/86	JW		800.00	PHX-396	2441	1,988,735.22	433,694.54 1,555,040.68
4/3/86	JM		5,100.00	ML-096	112	1,988,735.22	438,794.54 1,549,940.68
4/3/86	JM		2,953.96	ML-096	113	1,988,735.22	441,748.50 1,546,986.72
4/17/86	JM		800.00	ML-096	114	1,988,735.22	442,548.50 1,546,186.72
5/2/86	JM	32,000.00		PHX-347	629 ML-096	2,020,735.22	442,548.50 1,578,186.72
5/2/86	JM		2,570.97	ML-096	115	2,020,735.22	445,119.47 1,575,615.75
5/2/86	JM		5,100.00	ML-096	116	2,020,735.22	450,219.47 1,570,515.75
5/27/86	BF		125,000.00	ML-096	121	2,020,735.22	575,219.47 1,445,515.75
5/27/86	JW		800.00	ML-096	119	2,020,735.22	576,019.47 1,444,715.75
6/6/86	BF		16,564.00	ML-096		2,020,735.22	592,583.47 1,428,151.75

ENDORSEMENT TO ACCOUNTANTS'
PROFESSIONAL LIABILITY POLICY

970-056429

In accordance with the terms of Condition 10 in the policy the total premium payable, for

the next anniversary period is $ 178.00 .

This endorsement forms a part of and is for attachment to the following described policy issued by the CNA/INSURANCE company designated therein, takes effect on the effective date of said policy, unless another effective date is shown below, at the hour stated in said policy and expires concurrently with said policy.

Must Be Completed		Complete Only When This Endorsement Is Not Prepared with the Policy Or Is Not to be Effective with the Policy	
ENDT. NO.	POLICY NO.	ISSUED TO	EFFECTIVE DATE OF THIS ENDORSEMENT
#1	ACL 886 79 97	Robert Parris	5/1/74

CNA/insurance

Countersigned by ___Fred Daniel & Sons___
Authorized Agent

R1-40025-A

**Appendix III
Page 1 of 2**

CERTIFICATE OF INSURANCE

The Policy identified below by a policy number is in force on the date of Certificate Issuance. Insurance is afforded only with respect to those coverages for which a specific limit of liability has been entered and is subject to all the terms of the Policy having reference thereto including for Umbrella Excess Third Party Liability Insurance a provision requiring the maintenance of underlying insurance or self insurance. This Certificate of Insurance neither affirmatively nor negatively amends extends or alters the coverage afforded under any policy identified herein.

In the event of cancellation of the Policy the Company issuing said Policy will make all reasonable effort to send notice of cancellation to the Certificate Holder at the address shown herein, but the Company assumes no responsibility for any mistake or for failure to give such notice.

NAME AND ADDRESS OF INSURED
Robert O. Parris
111 East Choctaw
Sallisaw, Oklahoma   74955

NAME AND ADDRESS OF CERTIFICATE HOLDER

Oklahoma Education Department
School Finance Division
State Capitol Building
Oklahoma City, Oklahoma   73105

DATE OF CERTIFICATE ISSUANCE:

June 11, 1980

Fred Daniel & Sons
Authorized Representative

"Endorsements To 1986"

Original mailed;   June 11, 1980

THIS CERTIFICATE IS ISSUED AS A MATTER OF INFORMATION ONLY AND CONFERS NO RIGHTS UPON THE HOLDER

TYPE OF INSURANCE IS DESIGNATED BELOW	COVERAGES	LIMITS OF LIABILITY		
		EACH PERSON	EACH OCCURRENCE	AGGREGATE
I. ☐ Comprehensive Automobile Liability	Bodily Injury Liability	$	$	
☐ Basic Automobile Liability	Property Damage Liability		$	
	Bodily Injury and Property Damage Liability Combined		$	
☐ Uninsured Motorists	Uninsured Motorists	$	$ †	
I. ☐ Comprehensive General Liability	Bodily Injury Liability	$	$	$
☐ Owners', Landlords' and Tenants' Liability	Property Damage Liability		$	$
☐				
☐ Manufacturers' and Contractors' Liability	Bodily Injury and Property Damage Liability Combined		$	$
☐ Owner's and Contractor's Protective Liability				
☐ Beauticians' Malpractice Liability	Bodily Injury Liability	$	$	$
	Property Damage Liability		$	$
I. ☒ **COMPREHENSIVE ACCOUNTANTS LIABILITY**		**$100,000.00**		**$200,000.00**
V. ☐ Workmen's Compensation	A. Statutory	Statutory	Locations:	
Employers' Liability	B. Bodily Injury	$ †		
V. ☒ Umbrella Excess Third Party Liability	The Excess Insuror's Limit of Liability is (Complete one)			
	(a) $ **1,000,000.00** in excess of a Retained Limit			
	(b) Up to $_____ in excess of a Retained Limit			
	and in excess of various underlying Insuror's Limits of Liability			
	† each Accident			

Complete below, by designating company by number in the box and entering policy number and expiration date in the sections corresponding to the type of insurance indicated above.

I. ☐	II. ☐	III. ☐2 **ALL 985 75 57** 7/1/81	Policy Number Expiration Date
IV. ☐	V. ☐		Policy Number Expiration Date

☐1 Continental Casualty Company   ☐6 National Fire Insurance Company of Hartford   ☐8 American Casualty Company of Reading, Pa.

☐2 Transportation Insurance Company   ☐7 Transcontinental Insurance Company   ☐9 Valley Forge Insurance Company

G-32343-J

Appendix III
Page 2 of 2

LOAN RECORD CBT-1065

CUSTOMER

BOB PARRIS

DATE	NOTE NO.	COLLATERAL	AMOUNT	TOTAL AMOUNT DUE	LOAN RATE	OFFICER
-82	34273	Stock, R/E (Advance)	25,000.00	25,000.00	17½	bp
-82	34273	Stock,R/E(Advance)	58,000.00	83,000.00	17½	bp
-82	34273	" " " " " " " " " "	17,000.00	158,300.00	16	bp
-82	34512	F/S	58,300.00	158,300.00	16	bp
-18-83	35548	F/S	50,000.00	50,000.00	13½	bp
1-8-83	35548	F/S (Advance)	49,999.00	50,000.00	13½	bp
5-84	36168	F/S (Advance)	1.00	1.00	14	bp
0-84	36168	F/S (Advance)		70,001.00	CBT	bp
15-84	36722	Loan AgrmtmLife Ins,R/E				
23-84	36722	Furn,Fixt,Eqp (Advance)		72,029.00	BOK+1	bp
		" " " " " " " " "	90,000.00	132,029.00	BOK+1	bp
15-84	36722	" " " " " " " " " " "	67,972.00	200,000.00	BOK+1	bp
27-84	36168	F/S, (Advance)	90,000.00	290,001.00	CBT Pr	bp
16-84	36168	F/S (Advance)	10,000.00	296,119.95	CBT	bp
-85	36978	Inv,Furn,Fixt.Eqp.Life				
		Ins (Advance)	24,400.00	320,119.59	BOK+1	bp
-85	36978	" " " " " " " " " " "	8,000.00	328,381.34	BOK+1	bp
1-85	36978	" " " " " " " " " "	4,000.00	332,519.95	BOK+1	bp
1-85	36978	" " " " " " " " " "	3,000.00	333,946.31	BOK+1	bp
-85	36978	" " " " " " " " " "	15,000.00	209,547.51	BOK+1	bp
5-85	36978	" " " " " " " " " " "	20,000.00	329,547.51	BOK+1	bp
-85	36978	" " " " " " " " " "	4,999.00	334,546.51	BOK+1	bp
-85	37283	F/S, Equip, Grayhound	23,000.00	354,013.73	BOK+1	bp
		Dogs				
1-85	37352	R/E, F/S	55,250.00	384,515.75	BOK+1	jh
0-85	36168	F/S (Advance)	50,000.00	82,441.53	CBT	jh
6-85	36168	" " " "	7500.00	89,941.53	CBT	jh
12-85	36168	F/S (Advance)	13,000.00	69,941.53	CBT	jh
20-85	36168	F/S (Advance)	15,000.00	84,941.53	CBT	jh
04-85	36168	F/S (Advance)	15,000.00	94,941.53	CBT	JH
25-86	36168	F/S (ADV)	60.00	82,813.96	CBT	VC
3-86	36168	F/S (ADV)	104.4o	82,291.31	CBT	VC
24-86	36168	F/S (ADV)	179.00	81,143.45	CBT	VC
1-86	36168	F/S (ADV)	188.50	79,644.45	CBT	VC
1-86	36168	F/S (ADV)	138.00	55,373.93	CBT	VC
-17-86	36168	F/S (ADV)	1.00	54,536.43	CBT	VC
4-87	36168	F/S (ADV)	20.00	47,962.53	CBT	V C
-3-87	36168	F/S (ADV)	186.00	47,853.34	CBT	JH
-87	36168	F/S (ADV)	18.00	47,871.34	CBT	JH
0-87	36168	F/S (ADV)	28.00	47,661.72	CBT	JH
3-87	36168	F/S (ADV)	130.25	47,791.97	CBT	JH

Appendix IV

A copy of the

(6-3-86)

1	A Yes.
2	Q You were one of the plaintiffs in that lawsuit?
3	A Yes, sir.
4	Q As a trustee of this trust, do you recall whether
5	you all had assumed the duty to have an audit performed
6	of the trust every year?
7	A Yes.
8	Q Was an audit ever done?
9	A No.
10	Q Was never done during this period from 1980 to 1986?
11	A No, there wasn't.
12	MR. BRYANT: Thank you, Mr. Ford.
13	THE COURT: Thank you. Any redirect, Mr.
14	Condvertino?
15	MR. CONDVERTINO: Yes, sir, very briefly.
16	REDIRECT EXAMINATION
17	BY MR. CONDVERTINO:
18	Q Mr. Ford, you were cut off a couple of times and I
19	want to ask you about particularly the accounting bond.
20	Do you recall -- (Interruption)
21	A Yes.
22	Q -- being asked about the accounting bond? Were you
23	ever contacted by a representative of a bonding company
24	in order to reimburse you for the amount lost?
25	A No, sir, I wasn't.

Appendix V
Page 1 of 1

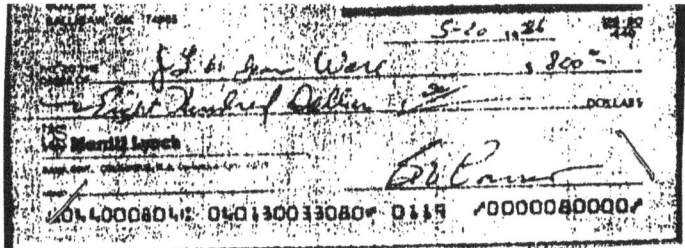

Appendix VII
Page 1 of 1

independent, with due deference accorded to the trial court's purely factual findings. (citations omitted) United States v. Montalvo-Murillo, 876 F.2d 826, 830 (10th Cir. 1989).

On August 29, 1991, defendant filed a Motion for Release Pending Appeal, copy attached. On the 16th day of September, 1991, plaintiff responded to defendant's motion, copy attached.   On October 16, 1992, the District Court held a hearing on defendant's motion.   On November 22, 1991, the District Court denied defendant's motion for release pending appeal by written Order, copy attached. Defendant/appellant now advances a pro se motion for immediate release pending appeal. This new motion assails the sufficiency of the evidence.

The evidence at trial proved, inter alia, that:

The $32,000 check received by defendant from Ms. Josephine Milligan was solicited and received April 29, 1986, and within the Statute of Limitations, as alleged in Count I of the Indictment.

Defendant participated in a telephone conversation with Jean Ware on June 20, 1986, and within the Statute of Limitations, in which he (defendant) falsely reported that the funds invested by the Wares were insured, that the Wares would be contacted by insurance officials, and that the Wares need not sue the defendant, consistent with the allegations in Count II of the Indictment.

Defendant sent an $800 check payable to Gerold Ware on May 20, 1986, and within the Statute of Limitations, to Mr. Ware by U.S. Mail, in furtherance of the scheme to defraud, which check was

doubt. He said: There's no doubt in my mind that check
was mailed. Now, the defendant wants us to believe that,
quote, somebody named Randy came down, picked up that
check, 32 grand, and drove it up to Fayetteville. That
was mailed. I leave it to your experience to decide
whether or not someone would give a $32,000 check to some
guy named Randy.

Count Two: Same plan here in all these counts.
Same plan to take these people's money by all counts.
June 20th, 1986. Mrs. Ware -- do you recall her
testimony -- called Mr. Parris from Dardanelle, Arkansas.
She called Oklahoma, do you recall? Mr. Anderson showed
her the telephone receipt and she recognized it and she
said: Yes, that's my number. Yes, that's going to his
number. I recall hearing his voice. I knew his voice.
That's called a wire fraud, wire transfer, the phone.

Count Three: May 20th, 1986, another mailing
from Mr. Parris in Oklahoma to the Wares in Arkansas.
That kept the Wares on the hook. That was an $800
interest payment. Kept them on the hook. Cash cow.

Now, our burden is reasonable doubt. We have
to prove the elements beyond a reasonable doubt. Not
beyond all doubt, but beyond a reasonable doubt. And,
that's based upon your reasoning and common sense when
you come to that. You recall the wizard never gave the

1 withdrawals from the trust?

2 A There was a little bit. Probably -- I don't

3 remember just what it was, but there was very little --

4 (Interruption)

5 Q How much?

6 A -- if any. I don't have any idea, you know, on

7 withdrawals.

8 Q You say a little amount?

9 A On the 60, I don't believe I withdrew anything on

10 the 60,000.

11 Q Then, you said you made a second investment in 1984.

12 And then during that period after 1984, did you make any

13 withdrawals after then?

14 A After 1984?

15 Q Yes, sir.

16 A There was two withdrawals, yes.

17 Q First withdrawal, what was the amount of that?

18 A Well, the first withdrawal was 90,000 to clear my

19 corporate notes and everything.

20 Q How did you get that $90,000?

21 A Bob wrote me a check for it.

22 Q Wrote it on the trust account?

23 A Yes.

24 Q Gave it to you?

25 A Yes.

Appendix IX
Page 1 of 2

1   Q   And then the second withdrawal, what was the amount

2   of that withdrawal?

3   A   Hundred and 25,000.

4   Q   When was that made?

5   A   That was made just before all this blew up.

6   Q   Just before the trust effectively had collapsed --

7   (Interruption)

8   A   Yes.

9   Q   -- is that correct?

10   A   Yes.

11   Q   How did you get that particular check?

12   A   Bob wrote the check.

13   Q   So, that would be a total of 215,000; is that

14   correct?

15   A   Well, I started with 400,000. Then, the 90,000

16   brought it to 310. And 125 off the 310.

17   Q   And then, you also testified that you recovered some

18   money after the trust collapsed. You didn't give an

19   amount. How much money did you recover out?

20   A   He wrote me a check right at the last for, I think,

21   like, $16,000.

22   Q   And, have you recovered any money since then?

23   A   No, sir.

24   Q   Mr. Ford, you brought a lawsuit of some kind against

25   Bob Parris, didn't you?

note
IT WAS #365,000
on 5/6-86

5-16.
not later on 2.

PARRIS MANAGEMENT TRUST

Account Balance:

5-17-86

Name	Deposited	Withdrew	Balance
Bob Parris	55,000.00	53,000.00	$ 3,000.00
Melba Denton	17,000.00	12,000.00	5,000.00
Carol Parris	35,000.00	15,000.00	20,000.00
J. O. Farmer	101,000.00	23,000.00	78,000.00
Ms. M.O. Parris	25,000.00	3,000.00	22,000.00
Paul Neville	30,000.00	20,000.00	10,000.00
Teague Estate	236,000.00	91,000.00	145,000.00
Jean Ales	8,000.00	7,000.00	1.000.00
Bill Brooks	40,000.00	none	40,000.00
Murel Copeland	1,700.00	none	1,700.00
Robert Suttle	34,000.00	7,000.00	27,000.00
Harrel Lee	40,000.00	none	40,000.00
Jean Ware	75,000.00	38,000.00	37,000.00
J. W. Milligan	424,000.00	186,000.00	218,000.00
James Jackson	167,000.00	79,000.00	88,000.00
Bill Ford Jr.	360,000.00	5,000.00	355,000.00
Bill Ford Jr.(cash)		148,000.00	(148,000.00)
Bill Ford Jr. (Stock - Cost)	324,000.00		(324,000.00)
Bill Ford Jr. (Balance)		17,000.00	(17,000.00)
TOTAL	1,649,000	1,047,000.00	602,000.00

figures rounded off to thousands

Doc. # 1

Appendix X
Page 1 of 1

Honorable Judge Seay: 5-31-91

        Please assign a different
attorney to my Case:

        Craig Bryant is a nice person,
but I don't feel that he is
capable of defending me properly—

                        Thank You

                        Bob Parris
                        Box 707
                        Sallisaw Ok. 74955
                        918 775-9286

RECEIVED

MAY 31 1991

WILLIAM B. GUTHRIE
CLERK, U. S. DISTRICT COURT

Note — AT THE HEARING
on June 3, 1991, the trial judge was told
~~that the~~ that the lawyer he had appointed
to defend me had (1) stipulated to two depositions
I had not seen, (2) stipulated to 75,500 government
documents that knowing their intended use, (3) my
lawyer had not corrected the errors in the indictment
(4) had not even looked at the ... errors in the indictment

Ex.161   **Appendix XI**
         Page 1 of 1

0-595-20536-4